The Calc Programming Language

Mark McIlroy

ISBN: 9798354449699

Independently published

Edition 7

Revised up to version 5.8 of the Calc language.

To access the Calc system and additional resources go to:

`calc.aitkencv.com`

CONTENTS

1. Introduction

Calc is a general purpose programming language developed in 2022 by the author. The language is suitable for application development.

Calc can also be used for system-level code where performance is not highly critical, for example device drivers for a printer.

This book is an introduction to the language and covers all the features of Calc.

It is recommended that this book be read along with viewing the example programs and the standard library header file.

The Design goals of Calc are:

- Minimalism - to be easy to learn, read and maintain.
- Reliability – a stable compiler that produces stable code, with rare crashes in application code reduced or eliminated.
- Programmer productivity - true string, boolean, date and decimal data types and features to assist with locating bugs as quickly as possible.
- Performance - Calc is primarily a compiled language. However it can also run by an interpreter. Calc code compiles to C code which can be compiled by any C compiler. This approach generates faster programs than languages that are interpreted or use a virtual machine.
- Wide platform availability - Calc can run on any platform that has a C compiler.
- Reentrancy - all language structures and library subroutines should be reentrant, i.e. the output of a function should depend only on the parameters that are passed to it, not internally stored data from previous function calls or global variables. Reentrancy has benefits in program reliability and also means that a function can be called from different parts of a program, or from different programs, with overlapping timing and function correctly.
- Orthogonality - any token combination that makes practical sense should be compileable into correct working code. For example, the assignment operator a = b is valid for all types in Calc including objects and arrays.
- Memory corruptions should be reduced or impossible. This type of bug is time consuming to locate and can cause rare crashes that are never located. A long term goal of the development of the compiler is that memory corruptions should be impossible.

Calc has a number of unique features such as links, object and array assignment, a true decimal data type, and a lack of unstructured control flow statements.

<u>Language features</u>

- Strong type checking at compile time to detect errors in code and also enable improved performance.

- Compiling and checking the entire source file when called, avoiding crashes when rarely used code runs.

- A preference for English words, e.g. 'and', 'or' to make code more readable.

- Detection of common bugs, e.g. re-use of loop control variables in an inner loop, array bounds overflow, infinite loops, mixed 'and' and 'or' without brackets.

- Avoidance of language features to improve reliability: variant variables, variable length function arguments, pointer assignment to random values.

- Statement oriented rather than expression orientated to simplify the program code and make it more readable.

- Integer and boolean data types are completely separate in Calc. This avoids many bugs that are time-consuming to locate in other languages.

- Calc follows the principles of Structured Programming, which generally increases program reliability and makes code easier to maintain. Control flow is directed by statements such as 'if' and 'while' which operate on blocks of code. There are no unstructured control flow steps (such as 'break', 'continue' and early 'return' statements).

- Both compile-time and run-time error messages identify the line in the program source code where the error occurred.

- Calc programs do not require a run-time environment to be installed. This considerably simplifies distribution and updating of systems.

- Many modern languages have 'exceptions' for error handling. Calc intentionally does not handle errors in this way, errors need to be handled in Calc by setting the value of variables, such as a value that is returned from a function.

- A Calc program can detect almost all program errors that can produce a memory corruption, including:
    - Array bounds overflow.
    - Attempting to free a data block twice.
    - Attempting to access a data block that has been freed.
    - Attempting to access or free a link variable that is set to NULL_LINK.
    - Assigning a link value from a 'link to general' to a link of the incorrect type.
    - Link data types in different files with the same name but different members.

The name of the language is derived from the fact that the Calc project initially began as a project to develop a macro language for my online calculator.

However, I decided to take the opportunity to fulfil a long-held ambition and develop a full programming language that could be used in software development projects.

2. A simple program

The following program prints the numbers from 1 to 10.

```
include "stdlib.calch";

module_name sample_program;

module_type main;
```

```
link_module stdlib;


function int main( int argc, resizable array of
                                        string argv)
{
    var int i;

    for (i=1 to 10)
        print( i );
}
```

A description of this program line-by-line is:

```
include "stdlib.calch";
```

This include statement is used to read program code from another file. The "stdlib.calch" file contains declarations of the standard library, which contains approximately 500 functions.

```
module_name sample_program;
```

A name for this source code file. This is optional if the module is not linked to other modules in the program.

```
module_type main;
```

The type of the source file. Each project must have exactly one "main" type source file.

If this source code line is missing it defaults to "main".

If the calc project is a stand-alone project, it must have a 'main()' function which must be in the 'module_type "main"' file.

If it is linked into a larger system, there should be no 'main()' function however the project still needs a 'module_type "main"' file.

All other files in the project should have a module_type of "secondary".

```
link_module stdlib;
```

This line of code indicates that the project will be linked with the 'stdlib' module (standard library).

```
function int main( int argc, resizable array of
                                         string argv)
```

This line of code defines a function with the name "main". Each project must have exactly one function named "main", which is called by the system to start execution of the program.

The parameters to main, "argc" and "argv" contain the values, if any, passed on the command line when the program is called.

```
    var int i;
```

A computer program consists of variables and operations on those variables.

This line of code declares a variable named "i", of type "int" (i.e. a numeric value, whole numbers only).

```
    for (i=1 to 10)
```

This line of code specifies a "for" loop. For loops are used to repeat a section of program code.

In this example, the code following the "for" statement is repeated 10 times, each time setting the "i" variable to a new value increasing from 1 up to 10.

If more than one statement needs to be repeated, the statements should be enclosed in braces as below:

```
for (i=1 to 10)
{
        print( i );
        print( i * 2 );
}
```

In this example all the statements within the braces "{", "}" are repeated 10 times.

```
print( i );
```

This line of code prints a value to the output, followed by a newline.

For performance reasons the 'to' value of a for statement is only evaluated once, before the loop commences.

The 'for' statement is Calc is intentionally simple to enable code to be written more quickly, and to enable high-performance implementation.

More complex loop structures can be coded with the 'while' loop structure.

3. Global statements

The global statements in Calc can be included anywhere in a source code file, outside of function definitions.

The global statements are as below:

- Include "filename.calch";

As described in the previous section this statement is used to include program code from another file into the file being compiled.

- Comments

Calc supports two types of comments. Comments are items of text within a program file that are intended for a human reader and are ignored by the compiler.

    // text until end of line

The '//' token starts a comment, which continues until the end of the line.

        /*

        */

The "/*" token starts a comment which continues until a "*/" token is read.

These comments may be nested, for example:


```
/*
    Start comment
    /*
      A comment within the main comment
    */
*/
```


- module_type

As described in the previous section.

- module_name name;

As described in the previous section.

- link_module module1;

To combine multiple source code files into a single Calc project, follow this procedure:

1. Include a

    module_name "xxxx"

    statement at the top of each source code file, with a different name for each file.

2. In the main file, include a:

    module_type main;

    statement at the top of the file and a function:

    ```
    function int main( int argc, resizable array of string argv )
    {
    ....
    }.
    ```

3. In every other source code file, include a:

    module_type secondary;

    statement at the top of the file.

4. In the main file, include a

link_module modulename1;

statement at the top of the file for each of the secondary files.

- const

The "const" keyword specifies a constant value. It is generally good programming practice to use "const" statements wherever possible, especially when a value appears several times in different parts of a program.

For example:

```
const double PI = 3.14159;
```

The format of constants for each data type in Calc are:

Data type	Constant format
int, short_int, medium_int, byte	123
double, float long_double	123.56, 1.0e10
decimal	123456.12
hexadecimal constants (integer types)	0xFFFF
binary constants (integer types)	0b10010
string	"abcde"

The following escape sequences are recognised in strings:

\n	Newline
\r	Carriage return
\t	Tab
\"	Double quote
\\	Backslash

date	'2021-01-01' [must be 12 characters including the quotes. Year-month-day.]
time	'14:00:00' [must be 10 characters including the quotes. 24 hour time.]
datetime	'2021-01-01 14:00:00' [must be 21 characters including the quotes.]
bool	true, false

Numeric constants recognise the following operators:

constant-name ( ) + - * / ^

including arithmetic precedence.

String constants recognise the following operators:

constant-name ( ) &

All other constants must be direct constant values, or a previous constant name.

- type

User-defined types are declared at the global file level, see the following sections.

- function declarations

Functions must be declared earlier in the file before they are called, either by including the whole function or by declaring the function name and parameters, for example:

```
function int f1( int x1, int x2 );
```


- var

Variables may be declared at the global level, i.e. outside a function.

In these cases the data item will be available in any function throughout the system.

If a global variable is to be used in more than one source code file, it must be declared normally in one source file only and should be declared with the 'extern' keyword in each other source file that will access that variable.

For example:

File 1:

```
var int run_mode;
```

File 2:

```
extern var int run_mode;
```

File 3:

```
extern var int run_mode;
```

File 4:

```
extern var int run_mode;
```

4. Variables and data types

The simple data types in Calc are:

Integer types:	Integer, i.e. whole numbers only.

`byte`
`short_int`
`medium_int`
`int`
	On 64 bit systems the maximum value for the int type is a 19 digit number.
	
	Some library functions convert numbers to floating point which have a maximum precision of 15 digits.

Floating-point types:
 	
`float`
`double`
`long_double`
	Floating point numbers for scientific calculations, for example 10.50 or 1.23e20

`decimal`	A numeric data type for money calculations, not subject to rounding error for addition and subtraction. This type has two decimal places.
`string`	Items of text.
`bool`	Boolean, 'true' or 'false'.
`binary`	A block of binary data, e.g. a tree node, a JPEG image.
`date`	A date.
`time`	A time.
`datetime`	A point in time with a date and time component.

The ranges for the numeric types are:

byte	-128	to 127
short_int	-32,768	to 32,767
medium_int	-2,147,483,648	to 2,147,483,647
int	-9,223,372,036,854,775,808	to 9,223,372,036,854,775,807

float	10^{-38} to 10^{38}	with 7 digits of precision
double	10^{-308} to 10^{308}	with 14 digits of precision
long_double	10^{-4932} to 10^{4932}	with 19 digits of precision

If memory usage is not a critical issue, for maximum performance the recommended numeric data types are `int`, `decimal` and `double`.

For example

```
var double y;

y = 25.5;
```

This section of code declares a variable named 'y', and then sets it to a value of 25.5

The data types are described in more detail in the following chapters.

Calc also supports grouped data types, 'arrays' and 'object' types which are also described later.

Finally Calc supports 'links' which are an advanced usage and are described towards the end of the book.

Local variables can be declared anywhere in a function. They are available from the point that they are declared at, to the end of the function.

Variables declared outside a function are termed 'global variables'. These variables are available from the point that they are declared to the end of the source file, and in other source files if declared with the 'extern' keyword in the other source file.

In cases where there is a global variable and a local variable with the same name, two separate variables will exist. Within the function that the local variable is declared, references to that variable name will refer to the value of the local variable.

Variables can be given an initial value when they are declared.

For example:

```
var int x, y = 2;
```

If a variable is not initialised in the program, the compiler will generate code to set the initial value of variables as below:

Type	Initialisation on (the default)	Initialisations off
int	0	random value
short_int	0	random value
medium_int	0	random value
byte	0	random value
decimal	0	random value
float	0	random value
double	0	random value
long_double	0	random value
bool	false	random value
string	""	empty variable
date	NULL_DATE	empty variable
time	NULL_TIME	empty variable
datetime	NULL_DATETIME	empty variable
binary	empty variable	empty variable

This variable initialisation can be switched off with a compiler switch to improve the speed of performance-critical software.

5. Functions

Program code within Calc is grouped into "functions".

A function is a block of code which can be called from another location within the program.

All code within Calc, except for global statements, must be within a function.

An example of a function is:

```
function int f1( int x1, int x2 )
{
        var int i;

        i = 2;

        result = x1 * x2 * i;
}
```

```
Example usage:

        x = f1( 2, 3 );
```

A line-by-line description of this function is:

```
function int f1( int x1, int x2 )
```

This statement defines the start of a function named 'f1'. It specifies that the function returns an 'int' value, and that it takes two parameters, both of 'int' type.

If the function does not return a value it should be declared as a "void" type.

For example:

```
function void f1( int x1, int x2 )
```

```
var int i;
```

Variables within a function are called 'local' variables. They have a value only within the function that they are declared in.

In cases where there is a global variable and a local variable with the same name, the two variables may have different values. The local variable value will be used within the function where that variable is declared.

```
i = 2;
```

This statement sets the value of the variable "i" to 2.

```
result = x1 * x2 * i;
```

The reserved word 'result' is used to set the value that is returned from a function.

The variable `result` is pre-defined within a function, with the data type that is returned from that function, and can be used in the same way as other variables within a function.

In this example the return value of the function is set to the two parameters multiplied together, multiplied by the local variable "i".

```
x = f1( 2, 3 );
```

An example usage of this function, this line of code would set the value of the variable "x" to 12.

Calc supports recursion, meaning that a function can call itself. Recursion is used in many algorithms such as parsing and traversing structures such as trees.

Recusion can result in very simple functions, however mentally it can be difficult to follow. Imagine a chain of function calls where each function just happens to have the same name.

Functions can return any data type including object types and arrays.

If a function returns an object type or array it can be assigned to a variable or accessed directly.

For example:

```
x = function1( 2, 3 );

y = function1( 2, 3 )[20];

y2 = function2( 2, 3 ).dataitem1;
```

Calc variables passed to functions can be passed 'by value' or 'by reference'.

The difference between the two passing types is described below:

by reference

When a variable is passed by reference to a function, if the variable's value is changed within the function then the variable's value is also changed in the function that called it.

Only variable names can be passed by reference, expressions such as 'x + 2' cannot be passed by reference.

When a variable is passed by reference, it must have the exact type than the function is expecting.

Objects, fixed arrays and resizable arrays are always passed by reference.

by value

When a variable is passed by value, a copy of the variable is passed into the function. This means that if the variable is changed within the function being called, the variable's value is not changed in the function that called it.

Any simple value in Calc can be passed by value, including variables and expressions.

The two passing types are specified as follows:

```
y = f1( ref x );          // pass variable 'x' by reference

y = f1( val x );          // pass variable 'x' by value
```


If the keyword 'ref' or 'val' is not used, the following defaults are used:

By value   Simple variables except 'binary' type variables, links, expressions.

By reference   'binary' type variables, arrays, objects, resizable arrays.

Unlike most other programming languages, the specification of by-value or by-reference in Calc is made when a function is called, not when it is defined.

This method allows a function parameter to be passed by value in one part of a program, and by reference in another part of the same program.

Because 'by value' passing creates a copy of the variable's value, this should not be used if possible where the variable has a large size, such as a string which contains the contents of an entire file.

In these cases use 'f1(ref str);' for example to pass the variable by reference.

There is a compiler option to identify places in a program where this problem occurs.

Numeric types may be mixed when a variable is passed by value. For example, and 'int' variable or expression may be used when a 'double' type is expected.

Naming function call parameters

In cases where constants are used in function calls, the meaning of the value may not be obvious.

For example consider the code below:

```
project_forward( effective_date, client_id, 12, true );
```

In this code the meaning of the first two parameters is fairly obvious. However what do the '12' and 'true' represent?

To determine the answer to this the definition of 'project_forward()' must be looked up which can be time consuming if this happens hundreds of times.

This situation can also lead to bugs where code is changed incorrectly and the error is not immediately obvious.

To overcome these problems, function call parameters in Calc can be named.

For example the code below can be used in preference to the above example:

```
project_forward( effective_date, client_id,
                        number_of_periods=12,
                        accumulate_balances=true )
```

If this language feature is used then the names in the function call list must match the names in the function definition.

The 'name=' text is for information only, it cannot be used to change the order of the parameters in the parameter list.

6. Assignment operations

Variables are given a value using the "=" assignment operator.

For example,

```
x = 30;
```

In this example the value of the variable will be set to 30.

The expression on the right hand side of the "=" may include other variables, constants, operators and function calls.

For example;

```
x = (2 * PI * x2 + f1( 45, 50 )) / 2;
```

In addition to the "=" operator there are five other assignment operators:

```
+=    Add the result of the expression to the variable.
-=    Subtract the result of the expression from the variable.
*=    Multiply the result of the expression by the variable.
/=    Divide the result of the expression into the variable.
&=    Concatenate the string on to the end of the variable.
```

For example:

```
y += 20;
```

This statement would add 5 to the value of the variable y;

7. Control flow statements

Program execution in Calc starts at the top of a function, and continues down through each line of code unless redirected by a "control flow" statement.

There are ten types of control flow statement in Calc: "if", "while", "do", "for", "repeat", "switch", "scan_list", 'scan_list_keys', 'scan_list_data' and "scan_db".

"If" statement

An "if" statement is the most basic control flow statement in Calc, and executes a statement or set of statements if a condition is true.

For example:

```
if (x < 1)
    print( "x1" );
```

This statement will print the text "x1" if the value of the variable "x" is less than one.

A similar example with a block of code is shown below:

```
if (x < 1)
{
    print( "x1" );
    print( "x2" );
    print( "x3" );
}
```

In this example the "if" condition will apply to the block of code surrounded by the braces "{" and "}", i.e. all three print statements.

An "if" statement may also have an "else" component, which is executed if the condition is false.

For example:

```
if (x < 1)
{
        print( "x1" );
        print( "x2" );
        print( "x3" );
}
else
{
        print( "y1" );
        print( "y2" );
        print( "y3" );
}
```

"If" statements may be chained in a sequence, such as in the example below:

```
if (x < 1)
        print( "x1" );
else
if (x < 2)
        print( "x2" );
else
if (x < 3)
        print( "x3" );
else
        print( "x4" );
```

In this example only one of the "print" statements will be executed, depending on the value of the variable "x".

"While" statement

The "while" statement is the simplest and most flexible looping structure in Calc.

This statement repeats a block of code multiple times until the condition becomes false.

For example:

```
y = 1;
```

28

```
while (y <= 20)
{
    print( y );
    y = y + 1;
}
```

This code would print the numbers from 1 to 20, i.e. it would continually repeat the block of code until the variable "y" was not less than or equal to 20.

"Do" statement

The "do" control structure is similar to the "while" structure, except that the condition is at the end of the code block. This means that the code block is always executed at least once.

For example:

```
y = 1;

do
{
    print( y );
    y = y + 1;
}
while (y <= 20);
```

"For" statement

The "for" statement repeats a statement or block of code a specified number of times.

For example:

```
for (i=1 to 10)
    print( i )
```

This statement would repeat the "print" statement 10 times, setting the value of the control variable "i" to values from 1 through to 10.

A step size may also be specified, as in the example below:

```
for (x=35 to 45 step 0.5)
    print( i )
```

This statement would repeat the "print" statement 21 times, setting the value of the control variable "x" to values from 35 through to 45 in steps of 0.5.

The control variable must be a numeric type.

If the step size is not specified it defaults to +1.

The step size may be a negative number.

For performance reasons the "from", "to" and "step" values are only evaluated once, before the loop commences.

If the difference between the start and end values is not an exact multiple of the step size, the loop is interpreted as:

```
while (current_value <= end_value)   for positive step sizes

while (current_value >= end_value)   for negative step sizes
```

To avoid potential bugs the control variable cannot have its value altered inside the loop, and cannot be used as the control variable of an inner loop within the main loop.

'Repeat' statement

A repeat statement is applicable when a count of the number of times that the loop has executed is not required.

The syntax is:

```
repeat numeric-expression times
     statement
```

As with all language elements the 'statement' may be a single statement or multiple statements enclosed in braces '{', '}'.

For example:

```
repeat 10 times
     print( "12" );
```

A 'repeat' loop is slightly faster than a 'for' loop and so should be used where applicable.

"Switch" statement

A "switch" statement executes a statement or block of code depending on the value of an expression.

For example:

```
switch ( x )
{
     case 1:
          print( "1" );

     case 2:
          print( "2" );

     case 3, 5, 6:
     {
          print( "3" );
```

```
            print( "4" );
    }

    default:
            print( "5" );
}
```

This code has the following effect:

1. Check the value of "x". This may be a full expression.
2. If the value is 1, print "1".
3. If the value is 2, print "2".
4. If the value is 3, 5 or 6 print "3" then print "4".
5. If the value is none of the values above, print "5".

The "default" section of code is optional. If it is present it must be the last section in the "switch" statement, and it is executed if none of the other statements are true.

Each 'case' section runs a single statement. If multiple statements are required, they can be enclosed in braces '{' '}'.

All simple Calc data types can be used in 'switch' expressions.

'Scan_list_keys' statement

The 'scan_list_keys' statement is used to scan through the keys of the items in a list.

The 'scan_list_keys' statement repeats a statement or block of statements for each key in the list.

For example:

```
scan_list_keys( string_or_int_variable in
                                object_type_variable)
{
...
```

}

The 'object_type_variable' is the key item of the structure, and can be an aggregate expression such as x[35]. The 'string_or_int_variable' must be a simple variable name.

The scan_list statement has an optional direction parameter, to determine whether the scan is in ascending order or descending order of the keys.

// ascending order

```
scan_list_keys( string_or_int_variable in
                          object_type_variable, true)
{
  ...
}
```
// descending order

```
scan_list_keys( string_or_int_variable in
                          object_type_variable, false)
{

  ...
}
```

The direction parameter, if present, must be a boolean constant.

'Scan_list_data' statement

The 'Scan_list_data' statement is used to scan through the data items that have been inserted into a list.

The 'Scan_list_data' statement repeats a statement or block of statements for each data item in the list.

For example:

```
scan_list_data (link_variable in object_type_variable)
{
...
}
```

The 'object_type_variable' is the key item of the structure, and can be an aggregate expression such as x[35]. The 'link_variable' must be a simple variable name.

The scan_list statement has an optional direction parameter, to determine whether the scan is in ascending order or descending order of the keys.

// ascending order

```
scan_list (link_variable in object_type_variable, true )
{
...
}
```
// descending order

```
scan_list (link_variable in object_type_variable, false )
{

...
}
```

The direction parameter, if present, must be a boolean constant.

'Scan_list' statement

The 'scan' statement is used to scan through linked data structures, see the section on Linked Data Structures.

The 'scan' statement repeats a statement or block of statements for each item in a data structure.

For example:

```
scan_list (item_type_variable in object_type_variable)
{
...
}
```

The 'object_type_variable' is the key item of the structure, and can be an aggregate expression such as x[35]. The 'item_type_variable' must be a simple variable name.

The scan_list statement has an optional direction parameter, to determine whether the scan is in ascending order or descending order of the keys.

```
                // ascending order

scan_list (item_type_variable in object_type_variable,
                                                true )
{
...
}
                // descending order

scan_list (item_type_variable in object_type_variable,
                                                false )
{

...
}
```

The direction parameter, if present, must be a boolean constant.

'Scan_db' statement

The 'scan_db' statement is used to scan through a list of records returned from a database query.

For example:

```
var db_connection cxn;
var db_query_result result1;
var db_row data;
var string query;
var int i;

calc_mysql_init();

cxn = db_login( DATABASE_NAME, USERNAME, PASSWORD );

query = "SELECT * FROM client_details ORDER BY client_name
";

scan_db( result1, query, data, cxn, i )
{
    print( i & ": " & db_get_field_string( "client_name",
                                                data ) );
}
```

The scan_db statement comes in two forms:

```
scan_db( result result1,
         string query,
         db_row data,
         db_connection cxn )
or

scan_db( result result1,
         string query,
         db_row data,
         db_connection cxn,
         int i )
```

The only parameters that need to have a value before the loop executes are the second parameter, which is the query string, and the fourth parameter, which is the database connection.

The database must have been opened before the data access code is run.

The value of the 'data' parameter in this example will be set to the next record on each iteration of the loop.

If a counter variable is present, 'i' in this example, it will be set to 0 the first time the loop code executes, 1 on the next cycle and so on.

After the loop finishes the counter variable will have a value equal to the number of times that the loop has cycled through.

Each parameter except the query string must be a variable name.

As with 'for' statements, a control variable cannot be used as a control variable in an inner 'scan_db' or 'for' statement, and it cannot have a value assigned to it inside the loop.

Do not use this statement for update SQL queries such as INSERT or UPDATE statements.

8. Boolean expressions

All the control structures except switch operate on a "boolean expression".

A boolean expression is an expression that can have only one of two values: true or false.

For example:

```
if (x < 1)
```

This expression "x < 1" is true if the value of "x" is less than one, and false otherwise.

The relational and boolean operators are:

Expression	Effect

relational operators

```
x == y          true if "x" equals "y"
x != y          true if "x" is not equal to "y"
x < y           true if "x" is less than "y"
x <= y          true if "x" is less than or equal to "y"
x > y           true if "x" is greater than "y"
x >= y          true if "x" is greater than or equal to
                    "y"
```

boolean operators

```
x and y         true if "x" is true and "y" is also true
x or y          true if "x" is true or "y" is true or both
                    are true
x xor y         true if "x" is true and "y" is false, or
                    "x" is false and "y" is true
not x           true if "x" is false

x in {expr1, expr2, expr3,...}     true if "x" is equal to
                    any of the values in the list. Both
                    "x" and the list of values may be
                    full expressions.

x not in {expr1, expr2, expr3,...} true if "x" is not
                    equal to any of the values in the
                    list. Both "x" and the list of
                    values may full expressions.
```

For example

```
if (x < y and x > y2 and not eof)
    print( "x" );
```

The 'not' operator is a high-precedence operator. This means that:

```
if (not a or b )
```

Is parsed as `if ((not a) or b)`.

If this is not the required expression, brackets should be used.

For example:

```
if (not (a or b))
```

Calc supports a boolean data type for variables.

For example:

```
var bool eof;          // variable named "eof", of type
                                "bool"

eof = false;

while (not eof)
{
...
}
```

As boolean expressions have a value, the following code is valid:

```
var bool x;

x = y < 1;
```

In this statement, the expression "y < 1" evaluates to 'true' or 'false', and this value is set to the variable 'x'.

The equal '==' and not equal '!=' operators can operate on any simple data type.

The comparison operators '<', '<=', '>', '>=' can operate on numeric types, strings, dates, times and datetimes.

The 'in' operator

Calc includes a set operator. This is used as follows:

```
if (x in {1, 2, 3, 4} ) …
```

This evaluates to true if 'x' is equal to any item in the set.

To check for not in a set, use

```
if (x not in {1, 2, 3, 4}) …
```

This evaluates to true if 'x' is not equal to any item in the set.

Any simple data type can be used with the 'in' operator, and the set items may be full expressions.

The set operator may be faster than using multiple 'if – else' operators, and also makes the program code clearer.

9. Numerical data types

Calc supports eight numerical data types:

int	Integer type
short_int	Integer type
medium_int	Integer type
byte	Integer type
decimal	Fixed-point integer with two decimal places
float	Floating-point type
double	Floating-point type
long_double	Floating-point type

Integer types are numeric data type for whole numbers only (positive, negative or zero).

"decimal" is a data type that is suitable for money calculations. It has a fixed number of decimal places (two) and gives exact calculation results.

Floating-point types are used for scientific calculations and any calculations that require a fractional component, such as $x = y * 0.5;$

Floating-point types

'double' is the recommended floating-point type for general usage.

'double' values support numbers with decimal components, such as 100.1045982 Including an exponential value from approximately 10^{-38} to 10^{38}

The precision of double values used in Calc is approximately 14 digits.

Care should be taken when using "==" and "!=" on floating-point types as calculation results may not be exact.

For example, x = x + 0.2 repeated 10,000,001 times should equal 2,000,000.2

However, using double-precision floating point binary arithmetic this actually results in a value of 2,000,000.199678

This is because the floating point values are stored in binary format, and the value 0.2 does not have an exact representation in binary notation.

This effect is a fundamental limitation of floating point binary arithmetic.

In another example:

```
var double x, y;

x = 0.2;
y = 0.4;

if (2 * x == y)
        . . .
```

This example should result in 'true'. However, due to the rounding issue with numbers such as 0.2, if executed in code this code segment would result in false.

If the 'decimal' data type was used, the correct answer would occur.

Exact results also occur for integer data types, and floating-point values that are whole numbers.

To compare floating-point values use a tolerance, such as

```
if (mabs( x - y ) < 0.000000001)
```

Operators

The arithmetic operators are:

```
+           Addition
-           Subtraction
*           Multiplication
/           Division
^           x to the power of y
mod         Modulus
```

The Modulus operator means: "if x is divided by y as an integer division, what would the remainder be".

For example, 10 mod 3 equals 1, because 10/3 as an integer division is 3, and 10 - 3*3 equals 1.

This seemingly strange definition is actually extremely useful and is widely used in algorithms.

For example:

1. Determine whether a number is even or odd.

```
if (x mod 2 == 0)       // if x is an even number

if (x mod 2 == 1)       // if x is an odd number
```

2. Allocate a large set of numbers into a smaller number of buckets.

```
bucket_number = x mod 10;           // group numbers 'x' into
                                    // 10 buckets
```

Division

Attempting to divide a number by zero will generate a run-time error, which includes the source code file and line number where the error occurred.

Division of integer types is a special case. In many languages a division 1 / 5 results in 0, because integer types don't store fractional components. There is usually a warning however.

In Calc, division of integer types is converted to type 'long_double', which includes the fractional component.

In Calc this example would be 1 / 5 = 0.2, with the result of the division being a value of 0.2 with a type of 'long_double'.

Assignment to integer types

If a floating-point value is assigned to an integer type, the fractional part is truncated not rounded.

For example:

```
var int i;

i = 1.9;

print( i );
```

This code would print 1.

Literal values

Numbers appearing directly in a program are known as literal values.

If a numeric constant does not contain a decimal point it is interpreted as an 'int' type, and if it contains a decimal point it is interpreted as a 'double' value.

For example:

```
X = 1 / 3;
```

This will generate a warning of an integer division and a value of 0, as 1/3 truncated to an integer is 0.

To avoid this problem add a '.0' to the end of the number.

For example:

```
X = 1.0 / 3.0
```

Will generate x = 0.3333333.

Alternatively, the type of a numeric constant can be specified using the following text after the number

Type	Code	Example
byte	b	12b
short_int	si	12si
medium_int	mi	12mi
int	i	12i
float	f	12.34f
double	db	12.34db
long_double	ld	12.34ld
decimal	dc	12.34dc

Increment and decrement

The "++" operator means "add one to the variable's value".

The "--" operator means "subtract one from the variable's value".

For example

```
x = 1;

x++;
```

```
print ( x );
```

This code would print the value 2.

The increment and decrement operators may also be used in expressions. When the operator is after the variable name it adds or subtracts after the variable's value is read for the expression, and when the operator is before the variable name it performs the operation before the variable is read for the expression.

For example

```
x = 20;
y = 20;

print ( x++ );
print ( ++y );
```

This code would print the values 20 and 21.

10. Strings

Strings within Calc are variables holding items of text.

For example:

```
var string s1;

s1 = "abc";

print ( s1 );
```

This code would print the text "abc".

Fixed string values must be surrounded by double quotes.

The following escape sequences are recognised in strings:

\n	Newline
\r	Carriage return
\t	Tab
\"	Double quote
\\	Backslash

For example,

```
print( "abc\ndef" );
```

This would print "abc", then a newline (move to the next line), then "def".

Concatenating strings

The concatenation operator "&" combines the value of two strings.

For example

```
var string s1, s2;

s1 = "abc";
s2 = "def";

print( s1 & ":" & s2 );
```

This code would print the text "abc:def".

There is also a concatenation assignment operator "&=" which appends the value of the expression to the variable.

For example

```
var string s1;

s1 = "123";
```

```
s1 &= ":456" & ":78910";

print( s1 );
```

This code would print the text "123:456:78910".

Substrings

To divide strings into parts use the `sleft()`, `sright()`, `sright_from_pos()` and `smid()` library functions.

For example

```
var string s1;

s1 = "123456789";

s1 = sleft( s1, 4 );

print( s1 );
```

This code would print the text "1234".

`sleft( s, n )`   return the leftmost 'n' characters from the string.
`sright( s, n )`   return the rightmost 'n' characters from the string.

`sright_from_pos( s, start_pos )`   return the rightmost characters from the string, starting from and including the character at position 'start_pos'.

`smid( s, x, y )`   returns a substring from the string "s" starting at position "x", with length "y".

`schar( s, n )`   returns a one-character string from position 'n' in the string 's';

String positions start at 0, meaning the first character.

`slength( s )` returns the number of characters in a string.

schar() is slightly faster than smid() so it should be used in preference to smid() when a single-character string is required.

<u>Foreign language text</u>

Calc fully supports foreign language text.

Information read from text files and web page forms is assumed to be in ASCII or UTF-8 format.

This includes the full Unicode character set.

The string functions such as `sleft()` operate on Unicode code points.

In general this means that `sleft( str, 5 )`, for example, would return the left-most 5 printable characters from the string and `slength( str )` would return the number of printable characters in the string (including whitespace characters).

There are some exceptions such as the code for a flag of a country, which occupies two code points.

Foreign language characters can be included in source code files within double quotes if the source code file is saved in UTF-8 format.

The relational operators <, >, <= and >= are only effective on strings of ASCII characters.

11. Dates, times and datetimes

Calc includes data types for dates, times and a combined date-time.

The data type names are "date", "time" and "datetime".

The constant values should be surrounded by single quotes.

They are specified as:

'YYYY-MM-DD'	For date constants
'HH:mm:SS'	For time constants
'YYYY-MM-DD HH:mm:SS'	For datetime constants

Where

YYYY	means the year
MM	means the month
DD	means the day of the month
HH	means the hour, 0 to 23
mm	means the minute
SS	means the second

These types can be compared with the relational operators "==", "!=", "<", "<=", ">" and ">=".

Calculations with dates and times require the use of library functions such as dadd(), which adds a number of periods to a date.

For example,

```
var date d1;

d1 = '2022-01-01';

d1 = dadd( d1, "days", 9 );

print( d1 );
```

This code would print the value 2022-01-10, meaning the tenth of January 2022.

To format dates and times into required formats use the `dformat()`, `tformat()` or `dtformat()` c library functions.

For example:

```
var date d1;

d1 = '2022-01-01';

print( dformat( d1, "%e%i %B %Y ) );
```

This code would print "1st January 2022".

The `dformat()` function takes a definition of the format required with a large range of options.

Date variables can be set to NULL_DATE, NULL_TIME or NULL_DATETIME to indicate that the variable does not contain a valid value.

This is the case for example when retrieving data from a database and a date value is blank.

Timezones

To adjust for timezones, use the ddtadd() or ddtsub() to add or subtract the required number of hours to convert the datetime value into the required timezone.

These functions change the date if the other timezone is currently one day forward or behind.

For example,

```
var datetime dt;

dt = '2025-03-01 10:00:00';
```

```
print( ddtsub( dt, "hours", 14 ) );
```

This code would print the effective date for 14 hours behind, being:

```
2025-02-28 20:00:00
```

12. Type conversions

Calc is a strongly typed language. This is to detect and prevent bugs within source programs, and to enable high-performance implementation.

In general an expression must have the type that is required in that particular context.

For example, the values on the left and right side of an addition operator "+" must be numeric types.

When a value is passed to a function, it must be of the correct type.

There are a number of exceptions:

- The "print" function can print any simple data type.

- Numeric data types may be mixed, for example an "int" variable could be used where a "double" value is required. However, if a variable is passed to a function call as a byreference parameter, it must be the exact type that is expected by the function.

- Link variables can be declared as "link to general", which allows any type of link to be passed to a general purpose function.

If a type conversion is required a library function can be used such as `cstring_to_date( string str, string format )` which converts a text string into a date value.

Aggregate data types

Aggregate variables are data variables that contain several data items within one variable name.

For example, an 'array' is a data type that contains a set of data items, all of the same type.

The aggregate data types in Calc are:

Array   A collection of data items, all of the same type.

List   A collection of items which contain links to data variables, and which can be searched.

Resizable Array   A collection of data items, all of the same type (with a size that can be changed while the program is running).

Object   A collection of data items, which may each be of a different type.

13. Arrays

13.1. Fixed arrays

An array is a set of data items, all of the same type.

In Calc an array variable is declared using syntax similar to the below:

```
var array [index size 1, index size 2,...] of <datatype>
varname1, varname2, varname3 etc.
```

For example:

```
var array [100] of int x;
```

The example above defines a variable named "x", which is an array variable holding 100 items of type "int".

To access a specific value in the array, use syntax similar to the below:

```
y = x[25];
```

This line of code sets the value of "y" to element number 25 in the "x" array.

Index values start at 0, up to the number of items minus one.

Arrays may be passed to functions by reference, returned from functions, and copied using a statement similar to

```
x = y;   // whole array copy
```

An array may have multiple dimensions, as in the example below:

```
var array [100, 200, 100] of int x;

y = x[25, 35, 38];
```

In this example the value x[25, 35, 38] refers to a single item in the array.

By default Calc checks array references to ensure that the index values are not outside the bounds of the array. This option can be turned off to increase performance for in-house applications that are calculation-intensive.

All the aggregate data types in Calc are orthogonal. This means that an array, for example, can contain any data type, including other arrays.

An example of this is the following code:

```
var array [100] of array [200] of int x30;
```

or

```
var array [100] of link to array [200] of int x32;

x32[20] = new array [200] of int;

x32[20].[30] = 40;

print( x32[20].[30] );
```

If a chained data declaration contains links and/or resizable arrays, these must be given a value from left to right before the data items can be accessed (using 'new' and 'setsize' respectively).

Array size expressions

Fixed array declarations recognise constant integer expressions for array sizes.

The array dimension size can be composed of:

- Constants of type 'int' declared with the 'const' keyword.
- Integer numbers.
- The following operators: ( ) + - * / ^

Arithmetic precedence is recognised so 2 + 3 * 4 is parsed as 2+ (3 * 4).

For example:

```
var array [2 * (MAX_SECTORS + 3)] of double x;
```

13.2. Resizable arrays

Standard arrays in Calc have a fixed size. Calc also supports resizable arrays that can have their size changed while the program is running.

A resizable array is declared with a syntax below:

```
var resizable array of <datatype> varname1, varname2,
varname3,...;
```

For example:

```
var resizable array of int x;
```

The array size is set using syntax below:

```
setsize variablename <indexsize1, indexsize2, …>;
```

For example

```
setsize x <100, 200>;
```

Resizable arrays are accessed using the same syntax as fixed arrays.

For example:

```
y = x[25, 35];
```

If an array is resized and it already contains data, and the new array has the same number of dimensions as the old array, the current data is copied into the new array.

A resize operation can change the number of dimensions of the array, however in this case existing data is not copied into the new array.

Resizing a large array is a relatively slow operation and should only be performed when necessary.

When to use tmp[x, y, z] and when to use tmp[x][y][z]

It is intended that multidimensional arrays in Calc be accessed using the syntax tmp[x, y, z, ...];

These arrays can be declared using a syntax similar to the below:

```
var array [100, 100, 100] of double tmp;
```

However due to the flexibility of the data declarations, it is also possible to declare multidimensional arrays that can be accessed using an alternative syntax.

For example:

```
var array [100] of array [100] of array [100] of double
tmp;
```

```
tmp2 = tmp[x][y][z];
```

The choice between tmp[x, y, z] and tmp[x][y][z] depends on how the variable is declared.

Two system functions are available to assist with using resizable arrays:

array_number_of_dimensions(rarray);

This function returns the number of dimensions currently in a resizable array.

array_index_size(rarray, index_number);

This function returns the index size (number of elements) of index number 'index_number' in resizable array 'rarray'.

Index numbers start at one.

16. 'object' variables

Calc supports 'object' types. An object type is a data type which contains several data items, which may be of different data types.

For example

```
type x object
{
      int a;
      string b;
      array [100] of int y;
};
```

An object type may contain arrays, and arrays can contain object types.

The individual data items are accessed using the dot "." operator, such as in the example below:

```
type tx object
{
      int a;
      string b;
      array [100] of int y;
};

var tx v1, v2;

v1.b = "abc";
v1.y[20] = 30;

v2 = v1;            // whole object copy
```

Object types can be used anywhere in the program, such as as global variables, local variables, and parameters to functions.

Objects may contain other objects.

For example:

```
type x2 object
{
        int x3;
        string x4;
        object
        {
                int x5;
        } x6;
};

var x2 x10, x12;

x10 = x12;              // copy the whole structure
x10.x6 = x12.x6;        // copy the inner object only
```

14. Object Orientated Programming

Calc was initially a procedural language, and the standard library is mostly procedural.

Calc also supports Object Orientated programming.

This approach allows data items and functions that operate on them to be grouped into a single object;

For example

```
type x1 object
{
        int x;
        int y;
        function int f1( int x1 );
```

```
        function string f2( int x2 );
};
```

The functions within an object are called by placing a dot after the data variable, similar to below:

```
var x1 item1;
var int x;

x = x1.f1( 29 );
```

The data items within an object of this type are known as member variables, and the functions are known as member functions.

The member functions can be defined with the object as shown below:

```
type object x1
{
        int x;
        int y;
        function int f1( int x1 );
        function string f2( int x2 )
        {
            print( x2 );
        }
}
```

Alternatively a member function can be defined separately as shown below:

```
type object x1
{
        int x;
        int y;
        function int f1( int x1 );
        function string f2( int x2 );
}
```

```
function string x1:f2( int x2 )
{
        print( x2 );
}
```

Member functions can access data variables at four levels:

Local variables	Declared within a function
Function parameters	Passed through the function call
Member variables	Declared within an object
Global variables	Declared outside functions and objects

A member function cannot have a local variable, member variable or function parameter with the same name;

A global variable is accessed if there is no local variable, member variable or function parameter with the same name.

Inheritance

The current version of Calc does not support Object Orientated inheritance directly.

However class hierarchies can be built in Calc by manually adding entries into objects.

For example:

```
type level1 object
{
        int x;

        function void f1()
        {
                print( x );
```

```
        }
};


type level2 object
{
        level1 parent;
        int y;

};


var level2 x2;

x2.y = 45;
x2.parent.x = 30;
x2.parent.f1();
```

15. User-defined types

A type can be given a name in Calc using the 'type' keyword.

The syntax of a user-defined type is:

```
type type_name <data_type> ;
```

Any data type in Calc can be given a name with the 'type' keyword.

For example:


```
type tx object
{
        int a;
        string b;
```

```
};
```

The "type" declaration is a global statement and must not be inside a function.

Variables declared with a user-defined type can only be assigned to variables of the same type, and passed to functions that are expecting a parameter of that type.

With types that are array or object types, variables declared using the user-defined type name can be accessed normally, for example

Object types

```
type x2 object
{
        string varname1;
        int varname2;
};


var x2 x;

x.varname1 = "abcd";
```

Array types

```
type x3 array [100] of int;


var x3 x10;

x10[y] = 45;
```

When a type is defined that is a simple data type, the internal data can be accessed using the ".data" operator.

For example:

```
type table_key int;


var table_key a;

a.data = 25;
```

16. Bit operations

Calc supports "bit" operations. These operations use the "int" data type.

In computing, a "bit" is a binary value that can only have the values 0 or 1.

A "byte" is a collection of eight bits and is typically used to store a single text character.

The operations on bits are:

and	The result bit is set to 1 if both source bits are 1
or	The result bit is set to 1 if either or both source bits are 1
xor	The result bit is set to 1 if either source bit is 1, but not both are 1
not	The result bit is set to 1 if the source bit is 0

There are a range of library functions for bit operations on "int" values.

In general application programming, the most common usage of bit operations is to pass a set of options to a general function.

For example:

```
const int MENU_TYPE_OPTION1 = 0b1;
const int MENU_TYPE_OPTION2 = 0b01;
const int MENU_TYPE_OPTION3 = 0b001;
const int MENU_TYPE_OPTION4 = 0b0001;

var int options_selected;

options_selected = bit_or( MENU_TYPE_OPTION1,
MENU_TYPE_OPTION3 );

show_menu( "main_menu", options_selected );
```

Or alternatively

```
show_menu( "main_menu", bit_or( MENU_TYPE_OPTION1,
MENU_TYPE_OPTION3 ) );
```

To combine multiple values into a single result code similar to the following can be used:

```
x = bit_or( x1, bit_or( x2, x3 ) );
```

Number formats

Integer constant values in Calc can be entered in decimal, hexadecimal or binary formats.

Decimal format is the normal number format such as

```
20.28
```

Scientific notation is also supported, such as:

1.56e25

Binary digits are 0 or 1, for example

```
0b100100
```

Hexadecimal is a base-16 number system.

The digit holders for a hexadecimal number are:

Value	Hexadecimal digit
0	0
1	1
2	2
3	3
4	4
5	5
6	6
7	7
8	8
9	9
10	A
11	B
12	C
13	D
14	E
15	F

For example:

```
0xEF9E
```

This hexadecimal constant would have the decimal value:

E * (16*16*16) + F * (16*16) + 9 * (16) + E

= 14 * (16*16*16) + 15 * (16*16) + 9 * (16) + 14

= 61,342 (decimal)

17. Binary data

Calc supports a data type named "binary". This represents a block of binary data, such as an image file contents.

The standard library contains functions for setting and reading bits and bytes within a binary variable.

For example:

```
var binary b1, b2;

bset_size( b1, 100 );

bset_byte( b1, 10, 38 );

b2 = b1;

print( bget_byte( b2, 10 ) );
```

18. Links

Links are an advanced topic and most programs can be written without the use of links.

A link variable in Calc is a data variable that points to another data object. This is also known as holding the address of another object.

Link variables can be used to connect two object types to create linked structures such as linked lists and trees.

Link variables are also used to create data objects which are stored in linked structures.

This approach is used by the standard library functions for implementing lists.

The 'new' operator is used to create a new object of the type that the link points to.

The 'new' operator creates a data item, and returns a link to it.

For example:

```
type t_1 object
{
        int a;
        string b;
        link to t_1 next;
}


var link to t_1 x1, y1;

x1 = new t_1;              // create a new object of type "t_1"

x1..next = new t_1;       // create another new object,
                          //    pointed to by 'next'

y1 = x1..next;



free x1..next;            // releases the memory allocated to
                          // the object pointed to by x1.next
                          // and sets x1.next to NULL_LINK
```

In this example the double dot has this meaning:

1. Determine the address held in the variable
2. First dot – convert this address into data contents
3. Second dot – access a field of the object type.
4. Field name – the field name in the object to access

The example above creates two new objects of type "t_1", and links them together using the link variable "next".

69

Links are followed to their destination data item using the dot "." operator.

The general rules are, where 'a' is a link variable:

a   The address pointed to by 'a'.

a.   The contents of the data pointed to by 'a'.

The syntax for some common combinations, where 'a' and 'b' are link variables, are:

```
a = b;              // set 'a' to point to the same data object as 'b'

a. = b.;            // copy the contents of the object pointed to by 'b' into the
                    // object pointed to by 'a'

x = a.;             // Set the variable 'x' to the contents of a simple data type
                    // pointed to by 'a'

x = a..field1;      // Access the object field 'field1' that is pointed to by 'a'
                    // and copy this value into the variable 'x'

x = a.[20];         // Access an array element of the data pointed to by 'a'
                    // and copy this value into the data variable 'x'
```

Links can point to any data type.

For example:

```
var link to int x;

x = new int;

x. = 30;

print( x. );
```

In this example the dot operator "." Is used to follow the link to its destination, which in this case is a 'int' value.

In the following example, an array and a two-stage link is used to show the required syntax in this case:

```
var array [100] of link to link to int x2;

x2[20] = new link to int;

x2[20]. = new int;

x2[20].. = 31;

print( x2[20].. );
```

Another example uses a link variable to dynamically create an array:

```
var link to array [100] of string x;

x = new array [100] of string;

x.[20] = 45;

print( x.[20] );
```

The 'new' operator

The 'new' operator can create a data item of any data type in Calc. It has the value of a link to a data item.

For example:

```
function void function1( link to int x1 );

var y link to string;
var x link to object_type_1;

y = new string;
```

```
y. = "5678";

x = new object_type_1;

function1( new int );
```

A link variable can be set to NULL_LINK to indicate that it doesn't point to an object.

Link to general

Calc is a strongly typed language and all type issues are checked at compile time, with some exceptions.

General purpose functions that can store different link types can use the 'link to general' type.

For example:

```
var link to general link_ptr;
```

Any link type can be assigned to a link to general variable, and a link to general variable can be assigned to any link type.

This functionality is included to allow for general purpose library functions.

To access the data pointed to by a general link, two methods can be used.

Method 1)

Assign the value to a link variable of the correct type and then use that variable.

For example:

```
var link to general glink_ptr;
var link to node link_ptr;

glink_ptr = f1();

link_ptr = glink_ptr;

x = link_ptr.data_item;
```

Method 2)

Use the link type indicator operator, '{ type }'.

For example:

```
var link to general link_ptr;

x = link_ptr {link to node} .data_item;
```

The link type operator 'name { type }' is used to indicate to the compiler the type of object that a general link points to.

It has the format:

```
general_link_variable_name {link to <datatype>}.
                                        data_item_to_access
```

The variable name before the '{' symbol can be an aggregate expression such as x[40] and must have the type 'link to general'.

When to use a single dot and when to use a double dot

To access a data item within an object type, use a single dot.

To access a data item from an object that is pointed to by a link variable, use a double dot.

Freeing memory allocations

Once memory has been allocated using the 'new' operator, it is not released until the 'free' operator is called on a link to that memory location.

This is the case even when the data variable is unreachable, such as with a local variable after a function has ended.

An example of freeing memory:

```
function f1()
{
        var link to double x1;

        x1 = new double;

        x1. = 29;

        function2( x1 );

        free x1;
}
```

Links to static structures

In Calc a link can only point to a dynamically-created item, created using 'new'.

A link cannot point to a standard Calc variable using an 'address of' operator, as could be done in other languages such as C.

For example:

```
        var int i;
        var link to int k;
```

```
k = &i;              // NOT part of the calc language.

k = new int;         // valid Calc code
```

Links to static objects were considered, and in fact were briefly implemented, but were removed from the language in order to make it simpler. These constructs can also lead to a range of memory corruptions that are difficult or impossible to prevent.

19. Lists

Calc has a 'list' data type.

List variables contain a set of items. Each item in the list has two elements: A 'key', which identifies the item in the list, and a link, which can link to any data type.

Each item inserted into a list must have a unique key. Also, an empty string "" cannot be used as a key.

Keys of items in lists can be strings, integers, or binary type variables.

Creating a list

A list variable is declared as follows:

```
var list x;

x.create( 0 );
```

The parameter to 'create' is for future expansion and is not currently used.

Adding items to a list

Items are added to a list using the 'insert_s()', 'insert_i()' or 'insert_b()' member functions. For example:

```
var list x;
var link to double x1

x.create( 0 );

x1 = new double;

x1. = 45;

    // Add an item into the list, with a key of 'item1'.

x.insert_s( "item1", x1 );
```

Searching for an item in a list

To seach a list and determine whether an item is in it, use the 'key_found_s()', 'key_found_i()' or 'key_found_b()' member functions.

```
var list x;
var link to double x1

x.create( 0 );

x1 = new double;

x1. = 45;

x.insert_s( "item2", x1 );

print( x.key_found_s( "item2" ) );        // prints 'true'
```

```
print ( x.key_found_s ( "item3" ) );        // prints 'false'
```

To search a list and retrieve the object that the list item links to, use the 'search_s()', 'search_i()' or 'search_b()' member functions.

For example:

```
var list x;
var link to double x1, x2
var bool item_found;

x.create ( 0 );

x1 = new double;

x1. = 45;

x.insert_s ( "item1", x1 );

        // sets 'item_found' to 'true' and retrieves a link
        // to the variable created at x1.

x2 = x.search_s ( "item1", ref item_found );

print ( x2. );
```

Scanning through a list

Lists are maintained in Calc in a sorted order.

There are three ways in Calc to scan through a list.

The example code below shows all three methods.

```
var list x;
var list_item litem;
```

```
var link to string lstr;
var string key;


x.create( 0 );


        // insert three items into the list

lstr = new string;
lstr. = "a";
x.insert_s( "1", lstr );

lstr = new string;
lstr. = "b";
x.insert_s( "2", lstr );

lstr = new string;
lstr. = "c";
x.insert_s( "3", lstr );


        // scan through the keys

scan_list_keys( key in x )
{
        print( key );
}


        // scan through the data items

scan_list_data( lstr in x )
{
        print( lstr. );
}


        // scan through the list objects

scan_list ( litem in x )
{
```

```
        lstr = litem.get_data_ptr();

        key = litem.get_key_s();

        print( key & ":" & lstr. );
}
```

The 'scan_list_keys' statement

The ;scan_list_keys' operator will repeat a loop of code for each key in the list.

The 'scan_list_data' statement

The ;scan_list_keys' operator will repeat a loop of code for each data item that has been inserted into the list.

The 'scan_list' statement

The ;scan_list_keys' operator will repeat a loop of code, setting the first variable to 'list_item' objects.

Using the list_item object it is possible to retrieve the key, data item link, and statistics such as the number of duplicate keys for that item in the list.

All three scan operators may take an additional parameter (meaning 'ascending') to scan in reverse order.

For example:

```
scan_list_keys(s1 in x, false)
```

Lists where a key is not required

In some cases just a list of data items is required, the data items do not have a key.

In these cases the 'unique_items_in_list()' function may be used to indicate an integer key for each insert operation.

For example:

```
var list x;
var link to string lstr;


x.create( 0 );

lstr = new string;
lstr. = "a";
x.insert_i( x.unique_items_in_list(), lstr );

lstr = new string;
lstr. = "b";
x.insert_i( x.unique_items_in_list(), lstr );

lstr = new string;
lstr. = "c";
x.insert_i( x.unique_items_in_list(), lstr );
```

This code will have the effect of assigning an integer key to each item in the list in the sequence 0, 1, 2, 3 etc.

Integer keys

Keys are stored in Calc lists in a bitwise pattern. This means that for a sorted output of integer keys, the positive values will be returned in sorted order, followed by the negative values in sorted order.

If your integer keys contain negative and positive values, add a 'bias' to all values before inserting and scanning.

For example:

```
var list x;
var list_item x_item;

x.create( 0 );

x.insert_i( 10 + 1000, NULL_LINK );
x.insert_i( -20 + 1000, NULL_LINK );
x.insert_i( 30 + 1000, NULL_LINK );
x.insert_i( 40 + 1000, NULL_LINK );
x.insert_i( -10 + 1000, NULL_LINK );

scan_list (x_item in x)
{
        print( x_item.get_key_i() - 1000 );
}
```

This code would print -20, -10, 10, 30, 40.

Key-only lists

In some cases it is only necessary to store a list of keys. In these cases, pass NULL_LINK as the second parameter to 'insert_s()', 'insert_i()' or 'insert_b()'.

Duplicate keys

When an insert operation is performed and the key is already in the list, the following procedure is performed:

1. The value of unique_items_in_list() remains unchanged.
2. The value of total_items_in_list() increases by one.
3. The link in the list item is replaced by the link that is passed to the new insert function call.
4. A scan of the list returns one item only for the duplicated item.

Freeing lists

Once a list variable has been created, the memory allocated to the list is not freed until the program code explicitly frees it, even if the list variable is a local variable.

An example of freeing a list is shown below:

```
var list x;
var list_item x_item;
var link to double x1;

x.create ( 0 );


        // insert some 'double' values into a list

x1 = new double;

x1. = 35;

x.insert_s ( "item1", x1 );


x1 = new double;

x1. = 45;

x.insert_s ( "item2", x1 );


        // free the double variables that have been inserted
        // into the list

scan_list (x_item in x)
{
     x1 = x_item.get_data_ptr ();

     free x1;
```

```
    }


        // free all the list item data

x.free_list();



Advanced usage

As an example of an advanced usage of lists, the code below has a list that
contains another list as its data.


var list x;
var list_item x_item, x_item2;
var link to list x1;

x.create( 0 );

x1 = new list;

x1..create( 0 );

x1..insert_s( "item1", NULL_LINK );

x.insert_s( "item1", x1 );


scan_list (x_item in x)
{
     x1 = x_item.get_data_ptr();

     scan_list (x_item2 in x1.)
     {
          print( x_item2.get_key_s() );
     }
}
```

The following example of list variables should print the number 44 twice:

```
var list l1;
var link to int x1;

x1 = new int;

l1.create(0);

x1. = 44;

l1.insert_s( "abcd", x1 );


    // retrieve x1 as a return variable

x1 = l1.search_s( "abcd", true );

print( x1. );


    // print the value of the return value directly

print( l1.search_s( "abcd", true ) {link to int} . );
```

20. Conditional compilation

Calc supports conditional compilation. This allows different sections of code to be compiled/run depending on specified conditions.

For example

```
#if interpreter
// code here
```

```
// code here
// code here
#end
```

In the example above, the Calc code within the #if and #end keywords will only be compiled or run if the 'interpreter' runtime environment has been selected.

At present the pre-defined conditions are:

compiler	true if the code is being compiled
interpreter	true if the code is being run by the interpreter
embedded	true if the code is running in an embedded environment

Additional constants can be defined on the compiler/interpreter command line using the ':set_true=name=' and 'set_false=name' options.

Boolean expressions are supported, such as '#if x1 and not x2'.

A variable can be set within the code using the '#set' operator.

For example:

```
#set x1 true
#set x2 false

#if x1
//...
//...
#end
```

The #if and #end keywords can appear anywhere in the token stream they do not have to be at the start of a line.

An #else is supported. For example:

```
#if x1
//...
//...
```

```
#else
//...
//...
#end
```

Also, #if statements may appear inside other #if statements (known as nesting).

For example:

```
#if x1
//...
//...
#if x2
//...
//...
#end
//...
//...
#else
//...
//...
#end
```

#include and #set may be within #if, for example

```
#if var1
#include "x.calch";
#end
```

```
#if var1
#set var2 true
#end
```

21. Performance issues

Calc is a high performance language. The Wattleglen compiler produces a C program as its output, which can be compiled to a program that is comparable to Assembly/Machine code in speed.

However there are some constructs in the Calc language which can cause performance issues.

Fast operations

Operations with simple variables, for example:

```
y = x * z;
```

Accessing an array element (fixed arrays or resizable arrays);

```
y = x[i];
```

Accessing a 'object' member:

```
y = x.field1;
```

Function calls:

```
x2 = function1( x1 );
```

Passing variables to functions:

```
function int f1( int x );
```

Inserting an item into a list.

```
l1.insert_s( "item1", x2 );
```

Searching for an item in a list.

```
x2 = l1.search_s( "item1", ref found );
```

Slow operations

The following operations are supported by the language but can slow program execution:

Assignment of large arrays and large "object" types:

```
y = x;                 // where 'y' and 'x' are large arrays or large "objects".

f1( str );             // where 'str' is a large string, for example an entire file
                                use f1( ref str );
```

Returning values from functions that are large arrays or large "'objects":

```
function array [10000] of string f1( int x )
```

Other issues

Operations with integer values are faster than operations with 'string' values. For this reason, codes used within programs should be integer values not string values where possible.

Operations with arrays are generally faster than operations with 'list' data variables.

Compiler switches

For maximum performance in cases where stability is not important, such as solving complex problems in a laboratory setting, set the following compiler options:

:no_runtime_checks   Don't check for divide by zero, etc.

:no_array_bounds_checks   Don't check whether array indexes are within
                          bounds.

:don't_initialise_variables   Don't initialise integer, floating-point, decimal,
                              or bool variables, or arrays of these types.

22. Data type and declaration summary

The simple data types are:

int	Integer numbers
short_int	Integer numbers
medium_int	Integer numbers
byte	Integer numbers
decimal	Fixed-point numbers with two decimal places
float	Floating-point numbers
double	Floating-point numbers
long_double	Floating-point numbers
string	Items of text
bool	'true' or 'false'
date	Dates
time	Times
datetime	A date and time
binary	A block of binary data

The user-defined types are:

type type_name <data_type> ;

The aggregate data types are:

<simple-datatype>

<user-defined type name>

array [index_size1, index_size2,...] of <datatype>

resizable array of <datatype>

object { variablelist } ;

link to <datatype>

Examples:

```
var string s1;

var int i, j, k;

var link to string s2;

var resizable array of double x1;

var array [100] of resizable array of string x2;

var resizable array of array [100] of int x3;
```

23. Linked data items

Arrays and object types in Calc are stored contiguously in memory. This means that if an array or object type has 10 items, the 10 items are stored in a continuous set of memory locations.

Linked structures operate differently. A linked data structure is composed of objects, that are linked together with links.

The 'scan_list' statement can be used to scan through linked data structures, see the examples below.

```
scan_list (item_type_variable in object_type_variable)
{
...
}
```

23.1. Linked lists

'Linked lists' are suitable for storing lists of items. They only occupy the space required and do not need to be resized.

Linked lists can be used to accumulate a set of items and then scan through them for processing.

The Linked List data type is a very simple structure that has a number of advantages.

1. The memory usage is very low and is only that required for the items in the list.
2. The size of the list grows with usage and does not have to be specified in advance.
3. The insert and first/last/next/previous operations are very fast.

This structure has a 'search' function, however the search function is slow for lists of greater than 20 or 30 members, as it needs to search through every item in the list up to the correct one.

Due to this the 'list' data type should be used for large lists where searching is required.


```
function void llnew( llist ll, int options );
```


Create a new linked list with initially no items. 'Options' is not currently used.


```
function link to llist_item llinsert( llist ll, string key,
link to general data_ptr );
```


Insert a new item into the list. The 'key' is optional and can be set to "" if searching for individual items it not required. The 'data_ptr' is a link to data to be stored in the list with this item. It can be set to NULL_LINK if only a list of keys is required.

```
function link to general llsearch( llist ll, string key );
```

Search the list for an individual item and return the link that was passed to the insert function call.

The 'llist_first_item()' and llist_next_item()' functions set the 'llist_current' value to the first/next item in a list. If 'ascending' is 'true', the items are returned in the order that they were inserted into the list. Otherwise the items are returned in reverse order to their insertion order.

Example

This example code creates a linked list, inserts the numbers 30 to 40 into the list, and then prints it.

```
type t_1 object
{
      int x;
};


function int main( int argc, resizable array of
string argv)
{

var llist ll;
var llist_current l_item;

var link to t_1 dat;
var int i;

      // create a list

llnew( ll, 0 );


      // create items and add them to the list
```

```
for (i=40 to 30 step -1)
{
    dat = new t_1;              // create new item

    dat..x = i;

    llinsert( l1, "", dat );
}


        // scan through the list

//******************************
// method 1: the 'scan' statement
//******************************


scan_list (l_item in l1)
{
    dat = l_item.ll_curr..data_ptr;   // .data_ptr is the
                                      // item passed to the
                                      // llinsert()

    print( dat..x );

    // or

    print( l_item.ll_curr..data_ptr {link to t_1} ..x );

}



//******************************
// method 2: direct function calls
//******************************


var bool continue_loop;


continue_loop = llist_first_item( l1, l_item, true );
```

```
while (continue_loop)
{
    dat = l_item.ll_curr..data_ptr;


    print ( dat..x );

      // or

print ( l_item.ll_curr..data_ptr { link to t_1} ..x );


    continue_loop = llist_next_item ( l_item, true );
}
```

Alternatively:

```
    print ( l_item.data_ptr {link to t_1} .x );
```

23.2. Bitstream trees

Bitstream trees are a new data structure that was developed as part of the Calc project. They can store items that are identified by a binary key.

A tree structure is useful when a large number of items need to be stored, with fast lookup of individual items, and also the ability to process the items in the tree in a sorted order.

Each item inserted into a Bitstream tree must have a unique key.

The maximum depth of an item in a Bitstream key is equal to the number of bits in the key, and in most cases is much less.

The 'list' data type in Calc is implemented as a Bitstream tree.

<u>Algorithm</u>

The basic concept of a bitstream tree starts with a key identifying the data item, such as an ASCII text string, Unicode text string, or an integer value.

Start from the first bit in the key, and take the left path down the tree if the bit is 0 and the right path if the bit is 1. Process the next bit, taking the left path for 0 and right path for 1 and so on. Continue until the full key has been processed and add the data item at that point.

In this basic structure every data item would be stored at a depth in the tree that is equal to the number of bits in its key.

The full implementation stores multiple bits at each level, so that the actual depth in the tree for each data item is generally much less that the depth associated with the basic model.

A bitstream tree is naturally balanced and does not require rebalancing after an insert operation.

24. Function examples

24.1. Sorting

The Calc standard library includes functions for sorting arrays of doubles, strings, and a general sort function.

These functions do not alter the input array, they work by creating a set of integer keys that are indexes into the input array.

For example:

```
        // create an array of doubles from the input
        // data

    for (i = 0 to num_items - 1)
        amounts[i] = items_today[i].amount;


        // generate the 'keys' array values
```

```
msort( amounts, keys, num_items_today, false );


        // can now refer to the input data in sorted order

for (i = 0 to num_items -1)
{
        j = keys[i];

        next_input_value = items_today[j].value;
}
```

If the sort comparison is more complex that a string or number comparison, for example if it requires comparing several fields in a structure, use the 'gsort()' Function.

This function can also be used for multi-key sorts.

For example, some data might need to be sorted by data value 'key1'. However where there are several items with the same value for 'key1', the data might need to be further sorted by 'key2', see below.

Key1	Key2
AAA	50
AAA	55
AAA	60
BBB	20
BBB	25
BBB	30
CCC	18
CCC	19
CCC	20

The comparison function must be declared using the 'function_table' operator.

It must have one argument, which is a link and have a return type of 'void'.

The comparison variable should be set to 1 if the first operand is greater than the second operand, -1 if the second operand is greater than the first operand and 0 if they are equal.

For example:

```
type x50 object
{
    int data;
};


function void fx2( link to gsort_item x3 )
{
      var link to x50 x1, x2;

      x1 = x3..item1;
      x2 = x3..item2;

      if (x1..data > x2..data)
           x3..compare_stat = 1;
      else
      if (x1..data < x2..data)
           x3..compare_stat = -1;
      else
           x3..compare_stat = 0;

}


function int main( int argc, resizable array of string argv )
{
var resizable array of link to x50 x1;
var resizable array of int keys;

setsize x1 <100>;
setsize keys <100>;

x1[0] = new x50;
x1[1] = new x50;
x1[2] = new x50;
x1[3] = new x50;

x1[0]..data = 100;
x1[1]..data = 50;
x1[2]..data = 20;
x1[3]..data = 200;


function_table fx2;
```

```
gsort( x1, keys, 4, "fx2", true );

print( x1[keys[0]]..data );
print( x1[keys[1]]..data );
print( x1[keys[2]]..data );
print( x1[keys[3]]..data );
}
```

24.2. Vectors

To perform operations with sets of numbers such as generating statistical analysis, use the "vector" data type.

For example:

```
var vector x, y;
var double correl;

vec_set_size( x, 10 );              // the vector size must be set
vec_set_size( y, 10 );              // before adding items

vec_set_item( x, 0, 1.1 );
vec_set_item( x, 1, 2.1 );
vec_set_item( x, 2, 3.4 );

vec_set_item( y, 0, 4.0 );
vec_set_item( y, 1, 5.2 );
vec_set_item( y, 2, 6.1 );


correl = st_correlation( x, y );    // calculate the
                                    // correlation between
                                    // the data sets

print( correl );
```

25. Databases

The standard library includes functions for accessing SQL databases.

This includes retrieving data and updating data in the database.

A database generally consists of a large number of 'records'.

Each record contains information such as customer details, product details, or an address history detail.

A 'table' is a collection of all records of the same type.

A 'column' is an individual field with a record such as customer ID, customer surname etc.

Information from one table to another is related using 'keys', which are normal data values that occur in more than one table.

A common example of a key could be 'Customer_ID'.

In this example, the Customer_ID value would appear in the primary customer table ("primary key"). It could also appear in other tables that have information that relates to a customer ("foreign key").

Almost all commercial databases at the current time use the relational data model, and can be accessed using the SQL language.

A separate book by the author, 'SQL Essentials', is a comprehensive guide to the SQL language.

Below is an example of an SQL query:

```
SELECT id, first_name
FROM customer_details
```

```
WHERE date_joined = '2022-01-01';
```

The below code example is a function for printing account codes and names from an accounting database.

```
function void print_accounts ()
{
        var db_connection cxn;
        var string query;
        var db_query_result result1;
        var db_row data;
        var int num_rows;
        var string account_code, account_name;

        cxn = db_login( "accounts", "USERNAME",
                                        "PASSWORD" );


        query = "SELECT * FROM accounts
                    WHERE active = 'yes' ORDER BY
                                        display_name";

        result1 = db_run_query( query, cxn );

        num_rows = db_query_num_rows( result1, cxn );

        repeat num_rows times
        {
            data = db_get_row( result1, cxn );

            account_code = db_get_field_string( "code", data
                                                );

            account_name = db_get_field_string(
                                    "display_name", data );

            print( account_code & ":" & account_name );
        }
}
```

26. Calling Calc code from a text string

The Calc standard libraries contain functions for calling the interpreter.

This allows a program to assemble a text string that contains valid Calc code, and execute it.

These functions can be called from compiled code, or code that is run using the interpreter.

The text string must contain a valid Calc program, including 'include' files and a main() function.

There are functions available to read and set global variables within this program, to put data into the text program and retrieve results.

27. A 2-page introduction to web pages

Calc can be used to produce online systems from a single web page, to complete systems.

Calc runs on the web server, not within the client browser.

To generate a web page, use the "output()" function.

Below is a brief introduction to HTML, CSS and AJAX items.

` `	Break, move to the start of the next line.
`<b>`	Start bold text.
`</b>`	End bold text.
`<i>`	Start italic text.
`</i>`	End italic text.
`<u>`	Start underline text.
`</u>`	End underline text.

Below is a simple table. <tr> stands for table-row and <td> stands for table-data (one cell in a table).

```
<table>
<tr><td class='AAA' style='BBB'>XXXX</td><XXXX</td></tr>
<tr><td>XXXX</td><XXXX</td></tr>
<tr><td>XXXX</td><XXXX</td></tr>
</table>
```

Below defines a style, which is referred to with the 'class=' option.

Values can be directly specified with the 'style='…'' option.

```
<style>
.text1    { color: #000000; font-family: verdana;
                font-weight: bold; font-size: 12pt }
</style>
```

Below prints some text in the specified style.

```
<span class='text1'>Sample text</span>
```

Below prints a link, which is some text that when clicked on causes the screen to jump to a new web page.

```
<a href='https://page-to-jump-to.com'>click on this
text</a>
```

Data entry forms use similar simple commands, starting with the `<form>` tag.

To show an image on a web page use:

```
<img src='/path/to/image/file' width=XX height=XX>
```

The below shows a method of updating a web page continuously, such as printing a clock, stock price or temperature on the screen that continually updates.

```
<span id='id1'>xxx</span>

<script>

function listen_text()
{
      var xmlHttp2;
      var s;

      xmlHttp2 = new XMLHttpRequest();

      xmlHttp2.onreadystatechange =

      function()
      {
          if (xmlHttp2.readyState==4)
          {
              if (xmlHttp2.responseText != "")
              {
                  s = xmlHttp2.responseText;

                  document.getElementById( 'id1'
                                    ).innerHTML = s;
              }
          }
      }


      var url = '/scripts/return_data_item.php';

      xmlHttp2.open('POST', url, true );

      xmlHttp2.send( null );
}

window.setInterval( \'listen_text()\', 1000);

</script>
```

The above commands can be used to generate simple web formatting for pages that are for internal use.

28. Reference information

<u>Lexical structure</u>

Calc code is free-format. Tokens are separated by whitespace, or one token ends where another begins.

All names and language keywords within Calc are case sensitive.

Names are used for variables, functions, types and constants.

A name within Calc cannot start with "_calcsys_" as this is reserved for compiler use.

To accommodate foreign languages, a name in Calc can be composed of any characters in the Unicode character set, except for the operator characters such as "=", whitespace characters, and cannot start with a digit.

Text for tokens is defined in language files and can contain apostrophes and underscores, but not spaces.

String constants can contain embedded newline characters. For example:

```
var string s1;

s1 = "
      Line 1 text
      Line 2 text
      Line 3 text
      ";
```

This is a valid string expression. The equivalent instruction using escape characters would be:

```
var string s1;
```

```
s1 = "\n\tLine 1 text\n\tLine 2 text\n\tLine 3 text\n\t";
```

Name conflicts

The following are the namespace rules:

a) The global namespace is composed of global variable names, function names, constant names and type names.

b) A global variable cannot be declared with a name that is already in use within the global namespace, or is a reserved word.

c) A function name cannot be declared with a name that is already in use within the global namespace, or is a reserved word.

d) A constant name cannot be declared with a name that is already in use within the global namespace, or is a reserved word.

e) A type name cannot be declared with a name that is already in use within the global namespace, or is a reserved word.

f) A type member cannot be declared with a name that is already in use within that type, is a type name, constant name, function name, or is a reserved word.

g) A function argument cannot be declared with a name that is already in use for a function argument of the same function, for a constant name, a function name, a type name or is a reserved word.

h) A local variable cannot be declared with a name that is already in use for a function argument of that function, a local variable with the same name in the same function, for a constant name, a function name, a type name or is a reserved word.

i) A function argument or local variable can be declared with a name that is the same as a global variable name.

Exceptions: the reserved word 'main' can be used as a module name and a function name.

Function declarations and definitions

Function parameter descriptions can occur in two circumstances: *declarations*, and *definitions*.

A function declaration has the function parameters followed by a semicolon. This is optional and may be used to declare the function before it is called.

Functions may be declared multiple times as long as the declarations are the same.

A function definition contain the function parameters, followed by the body of the function.

A function may only have one function body.

If a declaration is present it must match the definition.

Shortcut evaluation

Shortcut evaluation occurs when unnecessary elements of a boolean expression are not evaluated.

For example:

```
if (a or b or c())
```

In this case if a or b are true, the 'if' condition is true and there is no need to call function c().

To ensure consistent operation of programs, Calc compilers are required to implement shortcut boolean expression evaluation.

This includes shortcut evaluation for boolean expressions, 'switch' case expressions and the 'in' operator.

Include files

The keyword 'include' can be used to read input from another source code file.

The name after the 'include' must be a text string. It can be an internet address starting with 'https', a full path on the server starting with '/', or a filename.

If the include name is a filename only, the paths searched for the file must be specified on the compiler command line starting with ':I', for example ':Ipath-to-include-file'.

Loop variables

To avoid bugs and confusion loop variables such as 'for (i=0 to 100)' have some restrictions. A loop variable cannot be reused as a loop variable within an inner loop of the main loop, also the loop variable cannot have a value assigned to it inside the loop using an assignment '=' operator.

Function tables

Function tables allow a function to be called within a Calc program using a text string as the function name, or a function number.

This may be necessary when general library functions need to call a function from the user program.

Three steps are required to use this functionality.

1. Declare the functions that are available to be called by name in the main program, as below:

```
function_table f1, f2, f3;
```

2. Write the functions to be called. These must be void functions taking a single argument, a link type.

e.g.

```
function void f2( link to x x1 )
{
        print( x1.data_value );
}
```

3. Call the functions as required (by name).

```
call_function( link_variable, function_name_to_call );
```

```
e.g. call_function( x, "f2" );
```

This method of calling functions is slower than a direct function call "x = f1();" so should only be used when necessary.

4. Call the functions as required (by number).

```
call_function_by_number( link_variable,
function_number_to_call );
```

```
e.g. call_function_by_number( x, 1 );
```

The call function by number functionality is provided to allow the implementation of 'jump tables'.

The function numbers start at 0 upwards and are in the same order that the functions appear in the 'function_table' statement.

If a program has multiple 'function_table' statements, the functions are numbered from 0 upwards in the order that the compiler reads the statements.

A jump table is used to directly call a function from a long list of available functions, without having to search through the list using if-else or switch statements.

This method is comparatively fast and can be used as an alternative to a 'switch() / case' statement that has a very large number of 'case' alternatives.

As a link variable points to an object type which can contain multiple fields, these methods can pass multiple values into the function being called, and the function being called can return multiple values by setting variables within the object.

Collating sequences

String collating refers to the sort order of strings in Calc for list keys, the "<", ">", "<=" and ">=" operators, and the ssort() function.

English language characters are sorted as per the English alphabet, with 'A' coming before 'a' and 'aa' coming before 'aaa'.

Non-English characters are sorted as per their numeric value in UTF-8 format in the Unicode character set.

List of reserved words

The following words are reserved and cannot be used for variable names, function names, type names or constant names.

and	FALSE	mod	string
array	float	module_name	struct
binary	for	module_type	switch
byte	free	new	times
bool	function	not	to
call_function	function_table	of	true
call_function_by_name	general	object	TRUE
case	if	or	type
const	in	repeat	var
date	include	resizable	variable
datetime	int	scan_list	void
decimal	link	scan_db	while
default	link_module	secondary	xor
double	long_double	setsize	
else	main	short_int	

false   medium_int   step

The keywords 'false' and 'FALSE', and 'true' and 'TRUE' have the same meaning.

This is the list of reserved words for Calc programs written in English.

For Calc programs written in foreign languages, refer to the equivalent keywords listed in the

```
XXXX.calclanguage
```

file.

Expression types

When numeric data types are mixed in an expression, for example x + y, the result type of the expression is specified in the table below:

Note that if the operator is a division and both operands are integer types, then they are converted to long_doubles and the result of the expression is of type long_double.


```
Left Operand: int

Right Operand     Result Type

int               int
short_int         int
medium_int        int
decimal           decimal
byte              int
float             float
double            double
```

```
long_double      long_double
```

Left Operand: short_int

```
Right Operand      Result Type

int                int
short_int          short_int
medium_int         medium_int
decimal            decimal
byte               short_int
float              float
double             double
long_double        long_double
```

Left Operand: medium_int

```
Right Operand      Result Type

int                int
short_int          medium_int
medium_int         medium_int
decimal            decimal
byte               medium_int
float              float
double             double
long_double        long_double
```

Left Operand: byte

```
Right Operand      Result Type

int                int
short_int          short_int
```

```
medium_int        medium_int
decimal           decimal
byte              byte
float             float
double            double
long_double       long_double
```

```
Left Operand:      decimal

Right Operand      Result Type

int                decimal
short_int          decimal
medium_int         decimal
decimal            decimal
byte               decimal
float              double
double             double
long_double        long_double
```

```
Left Operand: float

Right Operand      Result Type

int                double
short_int          float
medium_int         double
decimal            double
byte               float
float              float
double             double
long_double        long_double
```

```
Left Operand: double

Right Operand      Result Type

int                double
short_int          double
medium_int         double
decimal            double
byte               double
float              double
double             double
long_double        long_double




Left Operand: long_double

Right Operand      Result Type

int                long_double
short_int          long_double
medium_int         long_double
decimal            long_double
byte               long_double
float              long_double
double             long_double
long_double        long_double
```

Standard library

In Calc, the standard library is considered part of the language. For example, Calc compilers can compile the bit functions bit_and(), bit_or() etc directly into system instructions to improve performance.

Dynamic memory allocation and freeing

Data items of any type, including arrays and objects, can be created using the 'new' keyword and deallocated using the 'free' keyword.

The following code will generate a run-time error:

- Attempting to free a data block twice.
- Attempting to access a data block that has been freed.
- Attempting to access or free a link variable that is set to NULL_LINK.

Since freeing a variable also sets it to NULL_LINK, the only way that system code might attempt to free a block twice (unintentionally) is by using code similar to the below:

```
var link to int x1, x2;

x1 = new int;

x2 = x1;

free x1;

free x2;
```

Link types

The compiler and interpreter check link types at compile time which should detect most program errors with incorrect types.

However there is also a check at run time to detect errors of the following types:

- Assigning a link value from a 'link to general' to a link of the incorrect type.
- Data types in different files with the same name but different members.

The run-time link type check does not use data type names so as to enable this check, a map of the data types within a definition is used.

The link type check applies to:

Dereferencing:	`x1.`
Assignment operation:	`x1 = x2;`
The link type operator:	`x1 {link to int} .`
Parameters passed to functions:	`f1( x1 )`

29. The Wattleglen Calc compiler

The Wattleglen Calc Compiler is the initial Calc compiler, also developed by the author.

The Wattleglen compiler is written in the Calc language itself.

The compiler produces a C program as its output which can be compiled and run on any platform that has a C compiler.

Information read from text files and web page forms is assumed to be in ASCII or UTF-8 format.

The compiler stores strings in a custom UTF-32 format. This format is a fixed-width format where every character occupies 4 bytes. The character representation is the UTF-8 value, padded with trailing zero bytes to make the four bytes.

This approach prioritises execution speed at the expense of higher memory usage.

A fixed-width encoding is specified to enable direct lookup of substrings, which is drastically faster than looking up substrings in variable length encodings such as UTF-8 and UTF-16.

Strings and 'binary' type values have a leading 8 byte value specifying the number of bytes in the string (excluding the leading 8 byte value).

Dates, times and datetimes are stored in ISO text format, such as

2022-01-01 08:30:00

All dates are stored in YYYY-MM-DD format, all times in HH:mm:SS and all datetimes in YYYY-MM-DD HH:mm:SS.

This approach is generally faster than converting date text to a numerical representation and back again.

If a numerical representation is required the function ddate_to_julian(date d1) can convert a date to the number of days since January 1 4713 BC.

Objects and arrays are a sequence of simple variables.

Resizable arrays have a header structure and a pointer to a sequence of variables.

Links point to a very small header structure that is retained in memory after the dynamic object is freed to enable the detection of double-frees etc.

Calc compilers should have array bounds checking (which can be switched off), and optional compiler initialisation of variables.

Memory management

Global variables, the 'new' operator and 'setsize' can access all available memory, up to the size of an 8 byte integer value (on 64 bit systems).

Local variables (variables declared within functions) access an area of memory known as the 'stack'.

The stack has a limited size, although this can be configured when the program is compiled.

The stack is not intended for storing large arrays.

Depending on the system that the program is operating on, you may not get a warning about potential stack overflow when the program is generated, the program may crash at runtime.

Large arrays should be declared as global variables, or declare the array as a resizable array and use setsize.

The Wattleglen compiler produces code that uses the following data sizes on 64 bit systems:

byte	1 byte
short_int	2 bytes
medium_int	4 bytes
int	8 bytes
decimal	8 bytes
float	4 bytes
double	8 bytes
long_double	12 or 16 bytes
bool	1 byte
string	152 bytes + 4 bytes per character for large strings
date	64 bytes
time	56 bytes
datetime	100 bytes
binary	24 bytes + 1 byte per byte in the item

Arrays and objects are stored contiguously in memory (i.e. in a continuous block).

For example:

```
type t_1 object
{
    int x;
    double x2;
    array [100] of int y;
};
```

Variables of this type would use 8 + 8 + 100 * 8 = 816 bytes of memory.

Execution speed and memory usage

The Wattleglen compiler was developed during a time when computer memory was plentiful and cheap.

For this reason most design decisions favour execution speed over memory usage.

Distribution

Calc does not require a runtime environment. The Wattleglen Calc compiler produces a C program as its output, which can be compiled along with the library routines to produce a single executable file for distribution.

The compiler itself can also run on any platform that has a C compiler.

C language interface

A Calc program can consist of multiple source files. Code within one source file can call functions from another source file, and access global variables from another source file, as long as the relevant declarations occur at the top of the source file and the source files are linked into an executable file with the system linker.

Calc code can call 'C' functions. Also, a 'C' program can call Calc code.

Refer to the documentation supplied with the system on how to do this.

Foreign languages

The Wattleglen compiler supports Calc source code written in foreign languages e.g. French.

The :osource_code_language_file=xxxxxx command line option can be used to specific the language of the source code file.

Language keywords and variable names should be in that language.

At present error messages are in English only.

To accommodate foreign language programs, a name in Calc is defined as any sequence of characters from the Unicode character set that are not operator characters (e.g. '='), whitespace characters (e.g. space, tab) and is not a language keyword.

A name can contain digits, 0 to 9 but cannot start with a digit.

Usage

```
calc_compile.exe calc-source-file.calc [options]
```

Calc-generated web page:

```
www.domain-name.com/run.php?file=calc-executable.exe
```

30. The Wattleglen Calc interpreter

The Wattleglen compiler set also includes an interpreter. Interpreters are slower than compiled code, however they have a number of advantages.

When debugging large systems, interpreted code can recommence immediately, after a program change, without the need to wait for a compile-link step which can take from seconds to minutes or more depending on the size of the system.

Also the interpreter can be embedded in applications, to build in a macro programming language into an application.

About the interpreter

The Wattleglen interpreter is written in C++.

Technically it produces icode instructions, which are then run by a run-time loop.

String handling is the same as the compiler. Strings are stored in a 4-byte format, which enables substrings to be directly located, without having to search the string as would be required in a UTF-8 or UTF-16 format.

In the interpreter, all simple variables are stored as a 'var' structure, which occupies 16 bytes of memory.

Arrays and objects are sequences of 'var' structures.

The same standard library is available in the interpreter and the compiler.

31. Standard library

The standard library of functions included with the system contains the following functions.

31.1.   Input/Output

function file_interface fopen(string filename, int mode, bool successful_open);

Opens a file for reading or writing. mode is one of:

FILE_MODE_READ
FILE_MODE_WRITE
FILE_MODE_APPEND

function string fgets(file_interface file_descriptor);

Reads a line from a text file up to a newline character, and returns the text as a string.

function void fputs(string s, file_interface file_descriptor);

Writes a string to a file, terminated by a newline character.

function bool feof(file_interface file_descriptor);

Returns true if reading from a file has reached the end of the file.

function void fclose(file_interface file_descriptor);

Close a file handle.

function bool fexists(string filename);

Returns true if a file exists.

function bool fis_a_directory(string pathname);

Returns true if a path exists and is a directory.

function datetime flast_modified_datetime(string filename);

Returns the last modified datetime of a file.

function int ffiles_in_folder(string pathname, resizable array of string filenames);

Generates an array of the filenames in a directory and returns the number of items found.

function void fdelete(string filename);

Deletes a file.

function int fsize(string filename);

Returns the size of a file.

function int fread(binary b, int number_of_bytes, file_interface file_descriptor);

Reads binary data from a file into a variable of type 'binary'. Returns the number of bytes read.

function void fwrite(binary b, int number_of_bytes, file_interface file_descriptor);

Writes binary data to a file.

function void fseek(file_interface file_descriptor, int pos);

Move the file read-write position to position 'pos'.

function int fcurrent_position(file_interface file_descriptor);

Returns the current file read-write position.

function string ffile_get_contents_text(string filename);

Read an entire text file into a string.

function string ffile_get_contents_binary(string filename, binary b);

Read an entire binary file.

function void mkdir(string dirname, int mode_bits);

Creates a new directory.

function void print(string s);

Prints a string expression. Use & to concatenate strings.

e.g. `print( "x: " & x & "y: " & y );`

function void output(string s);

Output a string expression without a newline. Use & to concatenate strings into a single value.

function string input_string();

Input a line of text from the console.

31.2. Strings

function int slength(string s);

Returns the length of a string.

function string sleft(string s, int length);

Returns the leftmost 'length' characters from the input string. If the 'length' value exceeds the length of the string then the entire string is returned.

function string sright(string s, int length);

Returns the rightmost 'length' characters from the input string. If the 'length' value exceeds the length of the string then the entire string is returned.

function string sright_from_pos(string s, int start_pos);

Returns the rightmost characters from the input string, starting at and including position 'start_pos'.

Positions start at 0.

If 'start_pos' exceeds the string length an empty string is returned.

function string smid(string s, int start, int length);

Returns a substring of 'length' characters from string 's' starting a position 'start'.

Positions start at 0.

If start_pos + length exceeds the string length the rightmost section of the string is returned starting at start_pos.

If 'start_pos' exceeds the string length a run-time error is generated.

function string schar(string s, int pos);

Returns a one-character string from position pos (starting at 0) from string s. This function is slightly faster than smid() so it should be used in preference to smid() when a single-character string is required.

function string stoupper(string s);

Returns an uppercase version of 's'. This function only operates on the characters 'a' to 'z', all other characters including foreign language text is left unchanged.

function string stolower(string s);

Returns a lowercase version of 's'. This function only operates on the characters 'A' to 'Z', all other characters including foreign language text is left unchanged.

function bool scaseieq(string s1, string s2);

Returns true if two strings are the same (case insensitive). Regular strings can be compared with "if (s1 == s2)".

function int ssearch(string s, string search_string);

Returns the position of the first 'search_string' within 's', or -1 if not found. Positions start at 0 meaning the first character.

function int srsearch(string s, string search_string);

Returns the position of the first 'search_string' within 's', searching from the end of the string backwards, or -1 if not found. Positions start at 0 meaning the first character.

function string strim(string s);

Trims whitespace characters (space, tab, \r, \n) from the start and end of a string.

function string sreplace(string s, string search_string, string replacement_string);

Returns a string from string 's' with all occurrences of 'search_string' replaced with 'replacement_string'.

function int sexplode(string s, string delimiter, resizable array of string receiving_array);

Breaks a string into sections using delimiter character 'delimiter'. Returns the number of items that the string was divided into.

The delimiter is generally a one-character string such as "~" etc however it may be a multi-character string.

Returns the number of items that the string was divided into.

function int sexplode_whitespace(string s, resizable array of string receiving_array);

Breaks a string into sections separated by one or more whitespace characters (space, tab, newline, carriage return).

Returns the number of items that the string was divided into.

function int sexplode_csv(string s, string delimiter, resizable array of string receiving_array);

Breaks a string into sections separated by a delimiter, usually a comma or a tab.

This function recognises quoted strings as a field value, for example:

```
aaa,"bbb,ccc",ddd
```

result =
```
        Field 1:            aaa
        Field 2:            bbb,ccc
        Field 3:            ddd
```

The quoted text may contain delimiter characters but should not contain a double quote.

Spaces are treated as ordinary characters, as part of a field value.

Returns the number of items that the string was divided into.

function int schar_to_int(string s);

Converts the first character in string 's' to a 4-byte UTF8 value (compatible with ASCII).

function string sint_to_char(int x);

Converts an integer ASCII or 4-byte UTF8 value into a one-character string.

function string text_is_valid_number(string text, int options, bool is_numeric);

Sets 'is_numeric' to true if 'text' represents a valid numerical string. Returns a cleaned version of the number, removing leading and trailing spaces and replacing '.xxx' with '0.xxx' and '-.xxx' with '-0.xxx'.

Values for 'options' are 0 or any combination of:

```
CHECK_NUMERIC_DISALLOW_NEGATIVES
CHECK_NUMERIC_DISALLOW_DECIMALS
CHECK_NUMERIC_ALLOW_SCIENTIFIC_NOTATION
```

Examples of valid numbers:

```
9
-9
9.9
-9.9
.9
-.9

9.9E9
-9.9E9
.9E9
-.9E9

9.9E-9
-9.9E-9
.9E-9
-.9E-9
```

This list contains all valid number formats recognised by this function, where '9' is a string of one or more digits.

function string iconvert_from_html(string text)

Converts a string containing HTML characters that have been encoded with iconvert_to_html() back to regular characters (e.g. ' is an apostrophe)

31.3. Mathematics

function double mrand();

Returns a random number between 0.0 and 1.0.

function void mseed_rand(int seed);

By default the random number generator will produce a different set of numbers each time a program is run. To produce a repeatable set of numbers, for example for debugging purposes, call mseed_rand(1) at the start of the program before calling mrand();

function int mtrunc(double x);

Truncates the decimal part of a number.

function double msqrt(double x);

Returns the square root of x.

function double mfabs(double x);

Returns the absolute value of double value 'x'.

function double mfmin(double x1, double x2);

Returns the minimum of two double values.

function double mfmax(double x1, double x2);

Returns the maximum of two double values.

function int miabs(int x);

Returns the absolute value of integer value 'x'.

function int mimin(int x1, int x2);

Returns the minimum of two integer values.

function int mimax(int x1, int x2);

Returns the maximum of two integer values.

function double mlog(double x);

Returns the logarithm of 'x' using base e.

function double mlog10(double x);

Returns the logarithm of 'x' using base 10.

function double mexp(double x);

Returns the value of e raised to the power of x .

function double mround(double x, int decimal_places);

Rounds a number to 'x' decimal places.

function string mformat(double x, int format, int decimal_places);

Formats a double number into a string.

Multiple format specifiers can be combined with '+' or bit_or().

Formats:

```
        // fixed number of decimal places
const int NUM_FMT_FIXED                 =    0b1;
```

```
        // floating decimal point, compatible with commas, trailing zeros are
truncated.

const int NUM_FMT_FLOATING              =    0b01;
```

```
        // for currency amounts, print either 0 or two decimals,
        // e.g. $12.1 is printed as $12.10, $14 is printed as $14
const int NUM_FMT_NEEDED                =    0b100;
```

```
        // print numbers as $xxx or -$xxx
const int NUM_FMT_CURRENCY              =    0b1000;
```

// Format in scientific notation with the specified number
// of decimal places, e.g. 1.234e10

const int NUM_FMT_SCI_NOTATION   = 0b10000;

// Do not commarise the output number
const int NUM_FMT_NO_COMMAS   = 0b100000;

function string miformat(int x, int format, int decimal_places);

Formats an int number into a string.

Multiple format specifiers can be combined with '+' or bit_or().

// print numbers as $xxx or -$xxx
const int NUM_IFMT_CURRENCY   = 0b1;

const int NUM_IFMT_NO_COMMAS   = 0b10;

function double msin(double x);

Returns the sine of x.

function double mcos(double x);

Returns the cosine of x .

function double mtan(double x);

Returns the tan of x.

function double marcsin(double x);

133

Returns the arcsine of x.

function double marccos(double x);

Returns the arccosine of x.

function double marctan(double x);

Returns the arctan of x.
function float mrandf();

Returns a random number between 0.0 and 1.0.

function int mtruncf(float x);

Truncates the decimal part of a number.

function float msqrtf(float x);

Returns the square root of x.

function float mfabsf(float x);

Returns the absolute value of float value 'x'.

function float mfminf(float x1, float x2);

Returns the minimum of two float values.

function float mfmaxf(float x1, float x2);

Returns the maximum of two float values.

function float mlogf(float x);

Returns the logarithm of 'x' using base e.

function float mlog10f(float x);

Returns the logarithm of 'x' using base 10.

function float mexpf(float x);

Returns the value of e raised to the power of x .

function float mroundf(float x, int decimal_places);

Rounds a number to 'x' decimal places.

function string mformatf(float x, int format, int decimal_places);

Formats a float number into a string.

Multiple format specifiers can be combined with '+' or bit_or().

Formats:

```
        // fixed number of decimal places
const int NUM_FMT_FIXED                =    0b1;

        // floating decimal point, compatible with commas, trailing zeros are
truncated.

const int NUM_FMT_FLOATING             =    0b01;


        // for currency amounts, print either 0 or two decimals,
        // e.g. $12.1 is printed as $12.10, $14 is printed as $14
const int NUM_FMT_NEEDED               =    0b100;

        // print numbers as $xxx or -$xxx
const int NUM_FMT_CURRENCY             =    0b1000;


        // Format in scientific notation with the specified number
        // of decimal places, e.g. 1.234e10

const int NUM_FMT_SCI_NOTATION         =  0b10000;


        // Do not commarise the output number
const int NUM_FMT_NO_COMMAS            = 0b100000;
```

function float msinf(float x);

Returns the sine of x.

function float mcosf(float x);

Returns the cosine of x .

function float mtanf(float x);

Returns the tan of x.

function float marcsinf(float x);

Returns the arcsine of x.

function float marccosf(float x);

Returns the arccosine of x.

function float marctanf(float x);

Returns the arctan of x.

function long_double mrandl();

Returns a random number between 0.0 and 1.0.

function int mtruncl(long_double x);

Truncates the decimal part of a number.

function long_double msqrtl(long_double x);

Returns the square root of x.

function long_double mfabsl(long_double x);

Returns the absolute value of long_double value 'x'.

function long_double mfminl(long_double x1, long_double x2);

Returns the minimum of two long_double values.

function long_double mfmaxl(long_double x1, long_double x2);

Returns the maximum of two long_double values.

function long_double mlogl(long_double x);

Returns the logarithm of 'x' using base e.

function long_double mlog10l(long_double x);

Returns the logarithm of 'x' using base 10.

function long_double mexpl(long_double x);

Returns the value of e raised to the power of x .

function long_double mroundl(long_double x, int decimal_places);

Rounds a number to 'x' decimal places.

function string mformatl(long_double x, int format, int decimal_places);

Formats a long_double number into a string.

Multiple format specifiers can be combined with '+' or bit_or().

Formats:

```
        // fixed number of decimal places
const int NUM_FMT_FIXED              =    0b1;
```

```
        // floating decimal point, compatible with commas, trailing zeros are
truncated.

const int NUM_FMT_FLOATING           =    0b01;
```

```
        // for currency amounts, print either 0 or two decimals,
        // e.g. $12.1 is printed as $12.10, $14 is printed as $14
const int NUM_FMT_NEEDED             =    0b100;
```

```
        // print numbers as $xxx or -$xxx
const int NUM_FMT_CURRENCY           =    0b1000;
```

```
        // Format in scientific notation with the specified number
        // of decimal places, e.g. 1.234e10

const int NUM_FMT_SCI_NOTATION       =  0b10000;
```

```
        // Do not commarise the output number
const int NUM_FMT_NO_COMMAS          =  0b100000;
```

function long_double msinl(long_double x);

Returns the sine of x.

function long_double mcosl(long_double x);

Returns the cosine of x .

function long_double mtanl(long_double x);

Returns the tan of x.

function long_double marcsinl(long_double x);

Returns the arcsine of x.

function long_double marccosl(long_double x);

Returns the arccosine of x.

function long_double marctanl(long_double x);

Returns the arctan of x.

31.4.   Dates & times

See also **cstring_to_date(string s, string format);**

This function creates a date variable from a text string. Format must be one of dd/mm/yyyy, mm/dd/yyyy, yyyy/mm/dd or yyyy-mm-dd

function date dtoday();

Returns the current date.

function time tnow();

Returns the current time.

function datetime dtnow();

Returns the current date & time as a datetime variable.

function string dformat(date d, string format);

Formats a date. Values in the 'format' string can be:

%a	Short weekday name	Sun
%A	Full weekday name	Sunday
%b	Short month name	Mar
%B	Full month name	March
%d	Day of the month (01-31)	19
%e	The 12-hour hour without leading zeros	2
%f	The day of the month without leading zeros	3
%H	Hour in 24h format (00-23)	14
%i	The English language suffix	1st
%I	Hour in 12hr format (01-12)	05
%m	Month as a decimal number (01-12)	08
%M	Minute (00-59)	55
%p	AM or PM	PM
%P	am or pm	pm
%S	Second (00-61)	02
%w	Weekday as a decimal number with Sunday as 0	4

%y	Year, last two digits (00-99)	01
%Y	Year	2012
%%	A % sign	%

function string tformat(time t, string format);

Formats a time value., see above.

function string dtformat(datetime dt, string format);

Formats a datetime value, see above.

function int dlast_day_of_the_month(int month, int year);

Returns the day number of the last day of the specified month. Months start at 1 for January. Year must be a 4-digit year.

function date dadd(date dt, string type1, int number);

Adds 'number' of periods of type 'type' to a date. Type1 is "day", "days", "month", "months", "year" or "years".

function time dtadd(time t, string type1, int number);

Adds 'number' of periods of type 'type' to a time. Type1 is "hour", "hours", "minute", "minutes", "second" or "seconds"

function datetime ddtadd(datetime dt, string type1, int number);

Adds 'number' of periods of type 'type' to a datetime. Type1 is "hour", "hours", "minute", "minutes", "second" or "seconds"

function date dsub(date dt, string type, int number);

Subtracts 'number' of periods of type 'type' from a date. Type1 is "day", "days", "month", "months", "year" or "years"

function time dtsub(time t, string type1, int number);

Subtracts 'number' of periods of type 'type' from a time value. Type1 is "hour", "hours", "minute", "minutes", "second" or "seconds"

function datetime ddtsub (datetime dt, string type1, int number);

Subtracts 'number' of periods of type 'type' from a datetime. Type1 is "hour", "hours", "minute", "minutes", "second" or "seconds"

function int ddiff(date dt_from, date dt_to);

Returns the number of days from date 1 to date 2, negative if date1 > date2.

function bool ddatestr_is_valid(string s, string format);

Returns true if the string 's' represents a valid date. Format must be one of dd/mm/yyyy, mm/dd/yyyy, yyyy/mm/dd or yyyy-mm-dd.

function bool dtimestr_is_valid(string s);

Returns true if the string 's' represents a valid time HH:MM:SS

function bool ddatetimestr_is_valid(string s);

Returns true if the string 's' represents a valid datetime YYYY-MM-DD HH:MM:SS.

function int dleap_year(int year);

Returns true if the year 'year' is a leap year.

function int dweekday(date dt);

Returns the day of the week of date 'date1', starting at 0 for Sunday

function int dday(date dt);

Returns the day of date 'd1' as an integer.

function int dmonth(date dt);

Returns the month of date 'd1' as an integer.

function int dyear(date dt);

Returns the four digit year from date 'd1' as an integer.

function int dhour(time t);

Returns the 24-hour hour from time 't' as an integer.

function int dminute(time t);

Returns the minute of time 't' as an integer.

function int dsecond(time t);

Returns the second of time 't' as an integer.

function int ddate_to_julian(date d1);

Returns the Julian date for 'dt', i.e. the number of days since January 1 4713 BC.

function date djulian_to_date(int jdate);

Converts a julian date to a YYYY-MM-DD date.

function date ddate_part(datetime dt);

Returns the date part of a datetime.

function time dtime_part(datetime dt);

Returns the time part of a datetime.

function date ddate_from_parts(int day, int month, int year);

Creates a date variable from its parts.

function time dtime_from_parts(int hour, int minute, int second);

Creates a time variable from its parts.

function datetime ddatetime_from_parts(int day, int month, int year, int hour, int minute, int second);

Creates a datetime variable from its parts.

function datetime ddatetime_from_vars(date dt, time t);

Creates a datetime variable from a date and time.

function string dparse_time(string text)

Converts a regular text date such as '2:30pm' into ISO format '14:30:00'.

To check for a valid text string use the regular expression:

([1-9]|10|11|12)(:[0-5][0-9])?(:[0-5][0-9])? ?(am|pm|AM|PM)

31.5. 'Binary' data type

function void bset_size(binary b, int len);

Set the size of a binary object.

function void bclear(binary b, int num);

Set a binary object to all values 'num'. Use after bset_size();.

function int bsize(binary b);

Return the number of bytes in a binary object.

function void bset_byte(binary b, int pos, int byte);

Set the byte at position 'pos'. Positions start at 0 upwards.

function int bget_byte(binary b, int pos);

Get the byte at position 'pos'. Positions start at 0 upwards.

function string bint_to_hex(int x, bool pad_with_leading_zeros);

Convert an integer to a string of hex digits.

function int bhex_to_int(string s);

Converts a string of hex digits to an 'int' type.

31.6. Database

function db_connection db_login(string database, string username, string password);

Login to a MySQL database and return a connection record.

function string db_prep_string_for_sql(string s);

Converts a text string into a suitable format for SQL by replacing apostrophes with double apostrophes. If this function is not used and the text contains an apostrophe then it will otherwise crash the SQL query.

function db_query_result db_run_query(string query, db_connection connection);

Run an SQL query and return a result record.

function int db_query_num_rows(db_query_result query_result, db_connection connection);

Returns the number of rows in a query result.

function bool db_query_has_rows(string query, db_connection connection);

Returns true if a query returns at least one row.

function db_row db_get_row(db_query_result query_result, db_connection connection);

Get the next row from a query result.

function void db_free_result(db_query_result query_result, db_connection connection);

Free the memory associated with a query result.

function bool db_field_is_null(string column_name, db_row row_data)

Returns true if a field value is NULL in a database record.

function bool db_field_is_in_query(string column_name, db_row row_data)

Returns true if the field 'column_name' exists in the query results.

function string db_get_field_string(string column_name, db_row row_data)

Get a single string data item from a query row.

function int db_get_field_int(string column_name, db_row row_data);

Get a single integer data item from a query row.

function decimal db_get_field_decimal(string column_name, db_row row_data);

Get a single decimal data item from a query row.

function double db_get_field_double(string column_name, db_row row_data);

Get a single double data item from a query row.

function bool db_get_field_bool(string column_name, db_row row_data);

Get a single boolean data item from a query row.

function date db_get_field_date(string column_name, db_row row_data);

Get a single date data item from a query row. If the database field is blank then the result matches NULL_DATE.

function time db_get_field_time(string column_name, db_row row_data)

Get a single time data item from a query row. If the database field is blank then the result matches NULL_TIME.

function datetime db_get_field_datetime(string column_name, db_row row_data);

Get a single datetime data item from a query row. If the database field is blank then the result matches NULL_DATETIME.

31.7.   Internet

function string iconvert_to_html(string text);

Convert a string into a format that is suitable for web browser display.

function string iurlencode(string text);

Converts a string into a format suitable for passing as a URL parameter, e.g. "abc def" becomes "abc%20def"

function string iurldecode(string text);

Decodes a URL string into a normal text string, e.g. "abc%20def" becomes "abc def"

function void ijump_to_page(string url);

Jump to another internet page. This function must be called before any printed output from the program.

function void iexit_if_search_bot();

Exit the process if the calling client is a search bot.

Include the file "calc_default_styles.calc" to use the default styles for text prompts, submit buttons etc.

function void write_HTML_headers(string page_title, string description);

Write the standard HTML headers to ensure that displays format properly on mobile phones.

31.8.   Forms

Include the file forms_library.calc to use these functions

function void form_text(string prompt, string name, int size, string init, int flags, string extra_text, db_connection cxn);

Display a text entry form field.

function void form_dropdown(string prompt, string name, string option_str, string init, int flags, string extra_text, db_connection cxn);

Display a dropdown list form field. The "option_str" should be in the format "<option>Value1</option><option>Value2/option><option>Value3</option>" etc.

To include a blank entry option start the option string with "<option></option>".

function void form_radio(string prompt, string name, string value, string desc, string curr, int flags, string extra_text, db_connection cxn);

Display a radio button form field.

The form will automatically select only one option from the options that have the same "name" value.

function void form_checkbox(string prompt, string name, string curr, int flags, string extra_text, db_connection cxn);

Display a checkbox form field.

function void form_textarea(string prompt, string name, int rows, int cols, string init, int flags, db_connection cxn);

Display a textarea form field, i.e. a text box with multiple lines.

function void form_password(string prompt, string name, int size, string init, int flags, db_connection cxn);

Display a password form field. The text entered will be shown as "*****".

function void form_submit (string form_name, string text, int width, db_connection cxn);

Display a form submit button.

function void form_end(db_connection cxn);

Call this function after "form_submit();".

function void show_link(string prompt, string page_to_jump_to, db_connection cxn);

Show a text link on a form.

31.9. Data type conversions

// Numeric conversions

```
<<external c>> function short_int      cint_to_short_int( int num );
<<external c>> function medium_int     cint_to_medium_int( int num );
<<external c>> function byte           cint_to_byte( int num );
<<external c>> function decimal        cint_to_decimal( int num );
<<external c>> function float          cint_to_float( int num );
<<external c>> function double         cint_to_double( int num );
<<external c>> function long_double    cint_to_long_double( int num );


<<external c>> function int            cshort_int_to_int( short_int num );
<<external c>> function medium_int     cshort_int_to_medium_int( short_int num
);
<<external c>> function byte           cshort_int_to_byte( short_int num );
<<external c>> function decimal        cshort_int_to_decimal( short_int num );
<<external c>> function float          cshort_int_to_float( short_int num );
<<external c>> function double         cshort_int_to_double( short_int num );
<<external c>> function long_double    cshort_int_to_long_double( short_int num
);


<<external c>> function int            cmedium_int_to_int( medium_int num );
<<external c>> function short_int      cmedium_int_to_short_int( medium_int
num );
<<external c>> function byte           cmedium_int_to_byte( medium_int num );
<<external c>> function decimal        cmedium_int_to_decimal( medium_int
num );
<<external c>> function float          cmedium_int_to_float( medium_int num );
<<external c>> function double         cmedium_int_to_double( medium_int num
);
<<external c>> function long_double    cmedium_int_to_long_double(
medium_int num );


<<external c>> function int            cbyte_to_int( byte num );
<<external c>> function short_int      cbyte_to_short_int( byte num );
<<external c>> function medium_int     cbyte_to_medium_int( byte num );
<<external c>> function decimal        cbyte_to_decimal( byte num );
<<external c>> function float          cbyte_to_float( byte num );
<<external c>> function double         cbyte_to_double( byte num );
<<external c>> function long_double    cbyte_to_long_double( byte num );


<<external c>> function int            cdecimal_to_int( decimal num );
```

```
<<external c>> function short_int          cdecimal_to_short_int( decimal num );
<<external c>> function medium_int         cdecimal_to_medium_int( decimal num );
<<external c>> function byte               cdecimal_to_byte( decimal num );
<<external c>> function float              cdecimal_to_float( decimal num );
<<external c>> function double             cdecimal_to_double( decimal num );
<<external c>> function long_double        cdecimal_to_long_double( decimal num );

<<external c>> function int                cfloat_to_int( float num );
<<external c>> function short_int          cfloat_to_short_int( float num );
<<external c>> function medium_int         cfloat_to_medium_int( float num );
<<external c>> function byte               cfloat_to_byte( float num );
<<external c>> function decimal            cfloat_to_decimal( float num );
<<external c>> function double             cfloat_to_double( float num );
<<external c>> function long_double        cfloat_to_long_double( float num );

<<external c>> function int                cdouble_to_int( double num );
<<external c>> function short_int          cdouble_to_short_int( double num );
<<external c>> function medium_int         cdouble_to_medium_int( double num );
<<external c>> function byte               cdouble_to_byte( double num );
<<external c>> function decimal            cdouble_to_decimal( double num );
<<external c>> function float              cdouble_to_float( double num );
<<external c>> function long_double        cdouble_to_long_double( double num );

<<external c>> function int                clong_double_to_int( long_double num );
<<external c>> function short_int          clong_double_to_short_int( long_double
num );
<<external c>> function medium_int         clong_double_to_medium_int(
long_double num );
<<external c>> function byte               clong_double_to_byte( long_double num
);
<<external c>> function decimal            clong_double_to_decimal( long_double
num );
<<external c>> function float              clong_double_to_float( long_double num
);
<<external c>> function double             clong_double_to_double( long_double
num );
```

// Conversions to string

```
function string cint_to_string( int num );
function string cdecimal_to_string( decimal num );
function string cdouble_to_string( double num );
function string cbool_to_string( bool x );
function string cdate_to_string( date dt, string format );
function string ctime_to_string( time t );
function string cdatetime_to_string( datetime dt, string format );
```

// Conversions from string

```
function int cstring_to_int( string s );
function decimal cstring_to_decimal( string s );
function double cstring_to_double( string s );
function bool cstring_to_bool( string s );
function date cstring_to_date( string s, string format );
```

creates a date variable from a text string. format must be one of dd/mm/yyyy, mm/dd/yyyy, yyyy/mm/dd or yyyy-mm-dd

```
function time cstring_to_time( string s );
function datetime cstring_to_datetime( string s );
```

// Conversions to/from binary

```
function string cbinary_to_string( binary b, bool output_as_hex );
```

convert a binary block into a text string. If 'output_as_hex' is true the output is hexadecimal digits, otherwise it is a text string ending at the length of the block.

```
function int cbinary_to_int( binary b );
function decimal cbinary_to_decimal binary b );
function double cbinary_to_double( binary b );
function date cbinary_to_date ( binary b );
function time cbinary to_time ( binary b );
function datetime cbinary_to_datetime ( binary b );
```

function binary cstring_to_binary(string s, bool input_is_hex);

> converts a text string to a binary object, either hex digits input or directly to binary.

function binary cint_to_binary(int num);
function binary cdecimal_to_binary(decimal num);
function binary cdouble_to_binary(double num);
function binary cdate_to_binary(date s1);
function binary ctime_to_binary(time s1);
function binary cdatetime_to_binary(datetime s1);

// Other type conversions

function datetime cdate_to_datetime(date dt1);
function string cbyte_to_string(int num);

> converts a single byte int value into a one-character numeric string

function int cstring_to_byte(string s);

> converts a one-character numeric string into an int value

31.10. Bit functions

The bit operations in Calc use the 'int' data type.

function int bit_and(int num1, int num2);

Bitwise AND of the bits in 'num1' and 'num2'.

function int bit_or(int num1, int num2);

Bitwise OR of the bits in 'num1' and 'num2'.

function int bit_xor(int num1, int num2);

Bitwise XOR of the bits in 'num1' and 'num2'.

function int bit_not(int num);

Bitwise NOT of the bits in 'num'.

function int bit_shift_left(int num);

Left shift one place of the bits in 'num' (filled with 0's).

function int bit_shift_right(int num);

Right shift one place of the bits in 'num' (filled with sign bits).

function bool bit_is_set(int num, int opt);

Returns true if the bit 'opt' is set in 'num', i.e. an AND operation is not zero.

'Opt' should be 0b1, 0b10, 0b100 etc.

31.11. Miscellaneous

function void msort(resizable array of double num, resizable array of int keys, int number_of_elements, bool ascending);

Sort an array of doubles. Sets an array of ints (keys). The values in this array are indexes into the original array of double values.

function void ssort(resizable array of string num, resizable array of int keys, int number_of_elements, bool ascending);

Sort an array of strings. Sets an array of ints (keys). The values in this array are indexes into the original array of string values.

<<external c>> function void gsort(resizable array of link to general num, resizable array of int keys, int number_of_elements, string compare_function_name);

General sort function. Sorts an array of links to any data type, using a user-defined sort function.

function int array_index_size(resizable array of int x, int index_nunber);

Return the size of an index of any resizable array. Index_numbers start at 1.

function int array_number_of_dimensions(resizable array of int x);

Return the number of dimensions of any resizable array.

31.12. System functions

function string syget_get_parameter(string parameter);

Returns a GET parameter, i.e. a value passed in a URL string such as:

```
www.address.com.au?param1=value1&param2=value2
```

function string syget_get_parameter_key(int num);

Returns GET parameter key number 'num'. Count starts at zero.

function string syget_get_parameter_value(int num);

Returns GET parameter value number 'num'. Count starts at zero.

function int syget_get_parameter_count();

Returns the number of GET parameters.

function string syget_post_parameter(string parameter);

Returns a POST parameter, i.e. a value passed into the program from a data entry form.

function string syget_post_parameter_key(int num);

Returns POST parameter key number 'num'. Count starts at zero.

function string syget_post_parameter_value(int num);

Returns POST parameter value number 'num'. Count starts at zero.

function int syget_post_parameter_count();

Returns the number of POST parameters.

function string syget_session_variable(string parameter, db_connection cxn);

Returns the value of a session variable. Session variables are used to pass data from one Calc web page to another Calc web page.

function void syset_session_variable(string parameter, string value, db_connection cxn);

Sets the value of a session variable. Session variables are used to pass data from one Calc web page to another Calc web page.

function void syexit(int exit_code);

Exit the current process. The exit code is passed to the shell calling the Calc program, and is generally 0 for normal exit and a number for an error code.

function string syget_ip_address();

Returns the IP address of the client.

function bool sylow_res_screen();

Returns true if the session is running on a low-resolution screen, generally a smartphone.

function void sydump_call_stack ();

Call this function when an error is detected in the program. This will print the call stack, i.e. the line number in each function that has been called, which will greatly aid debugging.

31.13. 'list' and 'llist' types

<u>'list' data type</u>

Each item inserted into a list should have a unique key. An empty string "" cannot be used as a key for a list item.

function void list : create(int options)

Creates a list. The 'options' parameter is for future expansion and is not currently used.

function int list : insert_s(string key, link to general data_ptr)

Insert an item into a list (with a string-type key). The 'data_ptr' parameter is a link type, linked to the data that is to be stored in the list.

Returns 0 for success and 1 for a duplicate key.

function int list : insert_i(int key, link to general data_ptr)

Insert an item into a list (with a int-type key). The 'data_ptr' parameter is a link type, linked to the data that is to be stored in the list.

Returns 0 for success and 1 for a duplicate key.

function int list : insert_b(binary key_bits, link to general data_ptr)

Insert an item into a list (with a binary-type key). The 'data_ptr' parameter is a link type, linked to the data that is to be stored in the list.

Returns 0 for success and 1 for a duplicate key.

function link to general list : search_s (string key, bool found)

Search a list for an item with the key 'key' (string-type key). This function sets the value of the 'found' parameter, and if found returns a link to the 'data_ptr' that was inserted into the list.

If not found this function returns NULL_LINK.

function link to general list : search_i (int key, bool found)

Search a list for an item with the key 'key' (int-type key). This function sets the value of the 'found' parameter, and if found returns a link to the 'data_ptr' that was inserted into the list.

If not found this function returns NULL_LINK.

function link to general list : search_b (binary key_bits, bool found)

Search a list for an item with the key 'key' (binary-type key). This function sets the value of the 'found' parameter, and if found returns a link to the 'data_ptr' that was inserted into the list.

If not found this function returns NULL_LINK.

function bool list : key_found_s (string key);

Returns 'true' if there is an item in the list with the key 'key' (string-type key).

function bool list : key_found_i (int key);

Returns 'true' if there is an item in the list with the key 'key' (int-type key).

function bool list : key_found_b (binary key_bits);

Returns 'true' if there is an item in the list with the key 'key' (binary-type key).

function bool list : delete_item_s (string key);

Deletes an item from a list (string-type key). Returns 'true' if the item was found.

function bool list : delete_item_i (int key);

Deletes an item from a list (int-type key). Returns 'true' if the item was found.

function bool list : delete_item_b (binary key_bits);

Deletes an item from a list (binary-type key). Returns 'true' if the item was found.

function bool list : first_item(list_item nptr, bool ascending);

This function sets the 'nptr' parameter to the first item in the list, in ascending or descending order.

Returns 'true' if there is at least one item in the list.

function bool list : next_item(list_item nptr, bool ascending);

This function sets the 'nptr' parameter to the next item in the list, in ascending or descending order, starting at current position 'nptr'.

Returns 'true' if the current item is not the last item in the list.

function int list : total_items_in_list();

Returns the number of items in the tree, including the count of duplicates if one or more items were inserted more than once.

function int list : unique_items_in_list();

Returns the number of items in the tree, counting each item once, regardless of duplicates.

function link to general list_item : get_data_ptr();

Returns the 'data_ptr' for a list item, which is the link that was passed to the 'insert' function call.

function string list_item : get_key_s();

Returns the key of a list item (string-type key).

function int list_item : get_key_i();

Returns the key of a list item (int-type key).

function binary list_item : get_key_b();

Returns the key of a list item (binary-type key).

'llist' data type (Linked List)

function void llnew(llist l1, int options);

Create a 'llist' variable. The 'options' parameter is for future expansion and is not currently used.

function void llinsert(llist l1, string key, link to general data_ptr);

Insert an item into a linked list. This function does not search the list for duplicates.

function link to general llsearch(llist l1, string key);

Search for an item in a linked list. This function returns the 'data_ptr' that was passed to the 'insert' function call, or NULL_LINK if the item was not found.

function bool llist_first_item(link to llist l1, link to llist_current l2, bool ascending);

Sets the 'llist_current' value to the first item in a list. If 'ascending' is 'true', the items are returned in the order that they were inserted into the list. Otherwise the items are returned in reverse order to their insertion order.

function bool llist_next_item(link to llist_current current_item, bool ascending);

Sets the 'llist_current' value to the next item in a list. If 'ascending' is 'true', the items are returned in the order that they were inserted into the list. Otherwise the items are returned in reverse order to their insertion order.

31.14. Vectors

function vector vec_set_size(vector x, int size);

Set the number of items in a vector. Existing data in the vector is preserved.

function int vec_get_size(vector x);

Return the number of items in a vector.

function void vec_set_item(vector x, int item, double value);

Sets an item in a vector.

function double vec_get_item(vector x, int item);

Returns an item from a vector.

function vector vec_add(vector x, vector y);

Add each element in 'y' to its corresponding element in 'x'.

function vector vec_subtract(vector x, vector y);

Subtract each element in 'y' from its corresponding element in 'x'.

function vector vec_multiply(vector x, vector y);

Multiply each element in 'y' by its corresponding element in 'x'.

function vector vec_divide(vector x, vector y);

Divide each element in 'y' into its corresponding element in 'x'.

function vector vec_square(vector x);

Square each element in 'x'.

function vector vec_sqroot(vector x);

Take the square root of each element in 'x'.

function vector vec_add_scalar(vector x, double y);

Add 'y' to each element in 'x'.

function vector vec_subtract_scalar(vector x, double y);

Subtract 'y' from each element in 'x'.

function vector vec_multiply_scalar(vector x, double y);

Multiply 'y' by each element in 'x'.

function vector vec_divide_scalar(vector x, double y);

Divide 'y' into to each element in 'x'.

function double vec_sum(vector x);

Return the sum of all elements in 'x'.

function double vec_average(vector x);

Return the arithmetic average of the elements in 'x'.

function vector vec_negate(vector x);

Reverse the sign of each item in vector 'x'.

function double vec_min_value(vector x);

Returns the minimum value in a vector.

function double vec_max_value(vector x);

Returns the maximum value in a vector.

function vector vec_sort(vector x, bool ascending);

Return a sorted vector.

function vector vec_clean_data(vector x, bool remove_negative_numbers, bool remove_zeros, bool remove_outliers, double outlier_num_of_standard_deviations, bool filter_out_low_values, double low_value_threshold, bool filter_out_high_values, double high_value_threshold);

Clean up a data set. If remove_outliers is true, any values more that 'outlier_num_of_standard_deviations' from the mean are removed from the result set.

function double vec_percentile(vector x, double percentile);

Return the percentile value from the data set. Percentile between 0.0 and 1.0, e.g. 0.9 for the 90th percentile.

function vector vec_continuous_var_frequency(vector x, int number_of_buckets, double step_size_per_bucket);

Returns a vector with the frequency of input values in each bucket. The 'step_size_per_bucket' does not need to be passed, it is a return value.

function vector vec_integer_variable_frequencies(vector x, vector x_without_duplicates);

Generates an array of distinct values, and returns a vector of the number of occurrences of each value.

31.15. Vectors of strings

function void vecs_set_size(vector_s x, int size);

Set the number of items in a vector.

function int vecs_get_size(vector_s x);

Return the number of items in a vector.

function void vecs_set_item(vector_s x, int item, string value);

Sets an item in a vector.

function string vecs_get_item(vector_s x, int item);

Returns an item from a vector.

function vector_s vecs_sort(vector_s x, bool ascending);

Sorts a string vector.

function vector vecs_process_duplicates(vector_s x, vector_s x_without_duplicates);

Generates an array of distinct strings, and returns a vector of the number of duplicates for each output string.

31.16. Statistics

function double st_linear_regression_slope(vector x, vector y);

Return the least-squares linear regression slope of x, y.

function double st_linear_regression_intercept(vector x, vector y);

Return the least-squares linear regression intercept of x, y.

function vector st_linear_regression_forecast(vector x, double slope, double intercept);

Calculate the y point on the line for each value in 'x'.

function double st_correlation(vector x, vector y);

Return the correlation on the values in x, y

function double st_stdev_p(vector x);

Returns the population standard deviation.

function double st_stdev_s(vector x);

Returns the sample standard deviation.

31.17. Finance

function double fin_general_calc(int calculation_type, double initial_amount, double final_value, double additional_amount_per_period, double additional_amount_growth_rate, double fund_growth_rate, int number_of_periods, bool solution_found);

General purpose financial calculator.

Usable for calculating loan repayments, retirement fund values, asset replacement funds etc.


```
const int FIN_CALC_CALC_INITIAL_VALUE        = 1;
const int FIN_CALC_CALC_FINAL_VALUE          = 2;
const int FIN_CALC_CALC_AMOUNT_PER_PERIOD    = 3;
const int FIN_CALC_CALC_INTEREST_RATE        = 4;
const int FIN_CALC_CALC_NUMBER_OF_PERIODS    = 5;
```


int calculation_type	See above
double initial_amount	Positive, negative or 0
double final_value	Positive, negative or 0
double additional_amount_per_period	Amount added/withdrawn per period
double additional_amount_growth_rate	Percentage increase in the amount added/withdrawn per period, per period

double fund_growth_rate value per period (percent)	Interest rate/growth rate in fund
int number_of_periods	Number of periods
bool solution_found	Returns true if a solution was found

For loan calculations the amount added per period should have the opposite sign to the initial value.

31.18. Printed output

For printed output from Calc programs, the PDF format is recommended.

To use the PDF functions, create a PDF document with pdf_create(), write text to it with pdf_add_text(), then call pdf_save_to_file() to save the document to a file which the user can open to view or print.

Coordinates are in points (1/72 inch), origin is the top left corner, x is horizontal coordinate.

Fonts supported are: Courier, Courier-Bold, Courier-BoldOblique, Courier-Oblique, Helvetica, Helvetica-Bold, Helvetica-BoldOblique, Helvetica-Oblique, Times-Roman, Times-Bold, Times-Italic, Times-BoldItalic, Symbol, ZapfDingbats.

Colors are 32 bit integers:

```
color = bit_shift_left( alpha_value, 24 ) +
        bit_shift_left( red_value, 16 ) +
        bit_shift_left( green_value, 8 ) +
        blue_value;
```

alpha_value: 0 (opaque) to 255 (transparent)

red_value/green_value/blue_value: 0 to 255

```
const double A4_PAGE_HEIGHT = 841.8898;              // pt
const double A4_PAGE_WIDTH = 595.2756;               // pt
```

For example:

```
var link to t_pdf this_pdf;

this_pdf = pdf_create( A4_PAGE_WIDTH, A4_PAGE_HEIGHT, "", "", "",
                                                    "", "", "" );

pdf_set_font( this_pdf, "Helvetica" );

pdf_add_text( this_pdf, "Test text", 12, 35, 35 );

pdf_new_page( this_pdf );

pdf_save_to_file( this_pdf, output_filename );
```

function link to t_pdf pdf_create(double page_height, double page_width, string creator_text, string producer_text, string title_text, string author_text, string subject_text, string date_text);

function void pdf_set_font(link to t_pdf this_page, string font_name);

function void pdf_add_text(link to t_pdf this_page, string text, double font_size, double y_position, double x_position);

function void pdf_add_text_right_align(link to t_pdf this_page, string text, double font_size, double y_position, double x_position);

function void pdf_add_text_center_within_field(link to t_pdf this_page, string text, double font_size, double y_position, double x_position, double field_width);

function void pdf_add_text2(link to t_pdf this_page, string text, double font_size, double y_position, double x_position, int color, int truncation_type, double max_width);

Write a line of text. truncation_type: 0 (no truncation), 1 (truncate characters), 2 (truncate words). text is truncated to fit within 'max_width' unless 'truncation_type' is 0

function double pdf_add_text_wrap(link to t_pdf this_page, string text, double font_size, double x_position, double y_position, int color, double wrap_width, double line_spacing, double page_top_margin, double page_bottom_margin);

Write a paragraph onto a rectangular area of the page. Returns the new y position

function void pdf_new_page(link to t_pdf this_page);

function void pdf_save_to_file(link to t_pdf this_page, string filename);

function void pdf_set_as_portrait(link to t_pdf this_page);

function void pdf_set_as_landscape(link to t_pdf this_page);

function double pdf_get_text_width(link to t_pdf this_page, string font_name, string text, double font_size);

function void pdf_free(link to t_pdf this_page);

function string pdf_get_error(link to t_pdf this_page);

function void pdf_clear_error(link to t_pdf this_page);

32. Commentary

1. Calc variables are initialised at the start of the program execution (global variables) or at the start of the function code (local variables). This action has a small performance penalty but is designed to help produce more stable and robust program code.

In languages where variables are not initialised, such as C, each variable typically has a random value at the start of code execution. This means that if there is a bug in the program, a program can be run twice, with identical inputs, and produce different outputs. In these cases it is extremely difficult to reproduce a problem for debugging and bugs can remain in the program for years without being found.

2. Simple Calc variables are 'pass by value' by default as function parameters.

This feature of the language is a safety feature. If an application program calls an external library, the code in the external library cannot change the value of the application variables, unless the programmer specifically allows this by using the 'ref' keyword.

33. Complete program examples

<u>Example 1</u>

Listed below is a complete example program. This is a simple web based calculator for calculating repayments on a loan.

This consists of two source files, sample_program1.calc and sample_program2.calc

Sample_program1.calc

```
include "stdlib.calch";
include "calc_default_styles.calc";
include "forms_library.calch";

module_type main;

module_name sample_program1;

link_module stdlib;

link_module forms_library;


function void form_start( db_connection cxn, string handler );


function int main( int argc, resizable array of string argv )
{
    var db_connection cxn;

    write_HTML_headers( "Sample program", "Loan calculator" );

    output( "<style>" );

    calc_default_styles();

    output( "</style>" );

    cxn = db_login( "aitkencv_aitkencv", "XXXXXX", "XXXXXX" );

    output( "<br>" );
    output( "<br>" );
```

```
        output( "<table width='100%'><tr><td align='center'>" );


        form_start( cxn, "/run.php?file=sample_program2.exe" );


        form_text( "Amount", "amount", 12, "", 0, "", cxn );

        form_text( "Interest rate", "interest_rate", 12, "", 0,
            "% p.a.", cxn );

        form_text( "Years", "years", 12, "", 0, "", cxn );


        form_submit( "form", "Calculate", 110, cxn );

        output( "</table></td></tr></table>" );

        form_end( cxn );

        syexit( 0 );
}


function void form_start( db_connection cxn, string handler )
{
        output( "<form id='form' name='form' action='" & handler & "'
method='POST'><table style='border: 1px solid #bbbbbb; background:
#F8FbFF; border-radius: 10px'>\n" );
}
```

Sample_program2.calc

```
        include "stdlib.calch";

        module_type main;

        module_name "sample_program2";

        link_module "stdlib";


function int main( int argc, resizable array of string argv )
{
        var double amount, interest_rate, years;
        var double rate, repayment;

        write_HTML_headers( "Sample program", "Loan calculator" );

        amount = cstring_to_double( syget_post_parameter( "amount" ) );
```

```
interest_rate = cstring_to_double( syget_post_parameter(
                        "interest_rate" ) );

years = cstring_to_double( syget_post_parameter( "years" ) );

if (interest_rate == 0)
{
        print( "Please enter a non-zero interest rate." );

        result = 1;
}
else
{
        rate = (interest_rate / 100) / 12;

        repayment = amount / ((1 - (1 + rate) ^ (-(years*12)))
                        / rate);

        print( "Amount: $" & mformat( amount, NUM_FMT_FIXED
                        , 0 ) );

        print( "Interest rate: " & mformat( interest_rate,
                                NUM_FMT_FIXED, 2 ) & "%" );

        print( "Years: " & years );

        print( "" );

        print( "Repayments: $" & mformat( repayment,
                NUM_FMT_FIXED, 2 ) & " per month." );

        result = 0;
}
}
```

Example 2

Listed below is an example program using files and arrays. This program reads an input file and prints it out in reverse order.

```
include "stdlib.calch";

link_module stdlib;


const int MAX_INPUT_FILE_LINES = 100000;

var array [MAX_INPUT_FILE_LINES] of string text_lines;


function int main( int argc, resizable array of string argv )
{
        var int line_number, i;
        var file_interface fp;
        var bool successful_open;

        fp = fopen( "input_file.txt", FILE_MODE_READ,
                                        ref successful_open );

        if (not successful_open)
        {
                print( "Can't open input file: input_file.txt" );
                syexit( 1 );
        }


        line_number = 0;


        while (not feof( fp ))
        {
                text_lines[line_number] = fgets( fp );

                line_number++;

                if (line_number >= MAX_INPUT_FILE_LINES)
                {
                        print( "Too many lines in the input file." );
                        syexit( 1 );
                }
        }


        fclose( fp );
```

```
        for (i=line_number-1 to 0 step -1)
            print( text_lines[i] );
}
```

34. Applications: Finite State Automata

A Finite State Automaton, also called a Finite State Machine, is a powerful programming technique that can reduce a variety of problems to simple sections of code.

This technique works by defining a 'state', which changes depending on a stream of input text or other conditions.

As an example a simplified version of the standard library function for checking whether input text is a valid number or not is shown below.

```
function bool text_is_valid_number2( string text )
{
        var int pos;
        var int len;
        var int state;
        var bool is_numeric;
        var string ch;
        var bool has_digit;

        is_numeric = true;

        has_digit = false;

        pos = 0;

        len = slength( text );

        state = 1;

        while (pos < len and is_numeric)
        {
                ch = schar( text, pos );

                if (not has_digit)
                {
                        if (is_digit( ch ))
                                has_digit = true;
                }

                switch (state)
                {

                                // first character
                        case 1:

                                if (ch == "-")
```

```
                                state = 2;
                        else
                        if (ch == ".")
                                state = 3;
                        else
                        if (is_digit( ch ))
                                state = 2;
                        else
                                is_numeric = false;


                        // string of digits before '.'
                case 2:

                        if (ch == ".")
                                state = 3;
                        else
                        if (not is_digit( ch ))
                                is_numeric = false;


                        // string of digits after '.'
                case 3:

                        if (ch == "e" or ch == "E")
                                state = 4;
                        else
                        if (not is_digit( ch ))
                                is_numeric = false;


                        // first character after 'e' or 'E'
                case 4:

                        if (ch == "-")
                                state = 5;
                        else
                        if (not is_digit( ch ))
                                is_numeric = false;
                        else
                                state = 5;


                        // string of digits after 'e' or 'E'
                case 5:
                        if (not is_digit( ch ))
                                is_numeric = false;

        }

        pos++;
}

if (not has_digit)
```

```
                is_numeric = false;

        result = is_numeric;
}


function bool is_digit( string ch )
{
        if (ch >= "0" and ch <= "9")
                result = true;
        else
                result = false;
}
```

35. Language grammar

Shown below is a full grammar for the Calc language.

The Calc language grammar is a LL(1) grammar, meaning that it can be parsed with a top-down parser using a one-token lookahead.

This grammar has one ambiguity, which is the if-else ambiguity.

The sequence 'if – if – else' can be parsed as 'if – (if – else)' or '(if – if) – else'.

As with most programming languages the Else is associated with the nearest If.


```
file:                          /* empty */
                           |   global_statement file
                           ;


global_statement:              TOK_MODULE_NAME
                               TOK_STRING_CONSTANT
                               TOK_SEMICOLON
                           |   TOK_MODULE_TYPE
                               TOK_STRING_CONSTANT
                               TOK_SEMICOLON
                           |   TOK_LINK_MODULE
                               TOK_STRING_CONSTANT
                               TOK_SEMICOLON
                           |   type_definition
                           |   const_declaration
                           |   variable_declaration
                           |   function_definition

                           ;


type_definition:               TOK_TYPE TOK_NAME datatype
                               TOK_SEMICOLON


type_variable_list:            datatype name_list TOK_SEMICOLON
                           |   datatype name_list TOK_SEMICOLON
                               type_variable_list
                           ;
```

```
name_list:                  TOK_NAME
                    |       TOK_NAME TOK_COMMA name_list
                    ;


const_declaration:          TOK_CONST TOK_INT TOK_NAME
                            TOK_ASSIGN constant-num-expression
                            TOK_SEMICOLON

                    |       TOK_CONST TOK_DECIMAL TOK_NAME
                            TOK_ASSIGN constant- num-expression
                            TOK_SEMICOLON

                    |       TOK_CONST TOK_DOUBLE TOK_NAME
                            TOK_ASSIGN constant- num-expression
                            TOK_SEMICOLON

                    |       TOK_CONST TOK_BOOL TOK_NAME
                            TOK_ASSIGN constant-boolean-expression
                            TOK_SEMICOLON

                    |       TOK_CONST TOK_STRING TOK_NAME
                            TOK_ASSIGN constant-string-expression
                            TOK_SEMICOLON

                    |       TOK_CONST TOK_DATE TOK_NAME
                            TOK_ASSIGN constant-date-expression
                            TOK_SEMICOLON

                    |       TOK_CONST TOK_TIME TOK_NAME
                            TOK_ASSIGN constant-time-expression
                            TOK_SEMICOLON

                    |       TOK_CONST TOK_DATETIME TOK_NAME
                            TOK_ASSIGN constant-datetime-expression
                            TOK_SEMICOLON


constant- num-expression:   add-expr
                    ;


constant-string-expression: num_expr
                    ;

constant-boolean-           TOK_BOOLEAN_CONSTANT
expression          |       TOK_NAME
                    ;

constant-date-expression:   TOK_DATE_CONSTANT
                    |       TOK_NAME
```

```
                                   ;

constant-time-expression           TOK_TIME_CONSTANT
                            |       TOK_NAME
                                   ;

constant-datetime-                 TOK_DATETIME_CONSTANT
expression                  |       TOK_NAME
                                   ;


datatype:                           datatype1
                            |       TOK_ARRAY TOK_LBRACKET
                                   array_index_size_list TOK_RBRACKET
                                   TOK_OF datatype
                            |       TOK_RESIZABLE TOK_ARRAY TOK_OF
                                   datatype
                            |       TOK_LINK TOK_TO datatype
                            |       TOK_OBJECT TOK_LBRACE variable-list
                                   TOK_RBRACE


                                   ;

datatype1:                          TOK_INT
                            |       TOK_SHORT_INT
                            |       TOK_MEDIUM_INT
                            |       TOK_BYTE
                            |       TOK_DECIMAL
                            |       TOK_FLOAT
                            |       TOK_DOUBLE
                            |       TOK_LONG_DOUBLE
                            |       TOK_STRING
                            |       TOK_BOOL
                            |       TOK_DATE
                            |       TOK_TIME
                            |       TOK_DATETIME
                            |       TOK_BINARY
                            |       TOK_NAME
                                   ;


array_index_size_list:              constant-num-expression
                            |       constant-num-expression TOK_COMMA
                                   array_index_size_list
                                   ;


function_definition:        |       TOK_FUNCTION function_return_type
                                   TOK_NAME TOK_LPARENTHESIS
```

```
                              function_parameter_list_all
                              TOK_RPARENTHESIS TOK_SEMICOLON

                    |         TOK_FUNCTION function_return_type
                              TOK_NAME TOK_LPARENTHESIS
                              function_parameter_list_all
                              TOK_RPARENTHESIS TOK_LBRACE stat_list
                              TOK_RBRACE
                    ;


                              TOK_VOID
function_return_type:    |    datatype
                    ;



                              /* empty */
function_parameter_list_all:  |  function_parameter_list
                    ;




                              function_parameter
function_parameter_list:  |   function_parameter TOK_COMMA
                              function_parameter_list
                    ;


                              datatype TOK_NAME
function_parameter:      ;

variable_declaration:    |    TOK_VAR datatype var_declaration_list
                              TOK_SEMICOLON
                    ;

var_declaration_list          var_declaration
                    |         var_declaration TOK_COMMA
                              var_declaration_list
                    ;


var_declaration               TOK_NAME
                    |         TOK_NAME TOK_ASSIGN constant_expr


                              TOK_SEMICOLON
```

```
stat:                            |    TOK_LBRACE stat_list TOK_RBRACE
                                 |    if_statement
                                 |    for_statement
                                 |    while_statment
                                 |    do_statment
                                 |    repeat_statement
                                 |    switch_statment
                                 |    scan_list_statement
                                 |    scan_db_statement
                                 |    free_statement
                                 |    function_table_statement
                                 |    call_table_function
                                 |    setsize_statement
                                 |    TOK_NAME function_call
                                 |    TOK_INC aggregate_expression
                                      TOK_SEMICOLON
                                 |    TOK_DEC aggregate_expression
                                      TOK_SEMICOLON
                                 |    aggregate_expression TOK_INC
                                      TOK_SEMICOLON
                                 |    aggregate_expression TOK_DEC
                                      TOK_SEMICOLON
                                 |    function_call TOK_SEMICOLON
                                 |    aggregate_expression assignment_right_side
                                      TOK_SEMICOLON
                                 |    variable_declaration
                                 ;


stat_list:                            /* empty */
                                 |    stat stat_list

                                 ;



setsize_statement:                    TOK_SETSIZE aggregate_expression TOK_LT
                                      array_index_size_list TOK_GT
                                      TOK_SEMICOLON
                                 ;

aggregate_expression:                 TOK_NAME dereference
                                 ;

dereference:                           /* empty */
                                 |    aggregate_expression TOK_LBRACE
                                      <datatype> TOK_RBRACE dereference
                                 |    TOK_NAME TOK_DOT dereference
                                 |    TOK_DOT TOK_NAME dereference
```

```
                              |      TOK_LBRACKET expression_list
                                     TOK_RBRACKET dereference
                              ;


expression_list:                     bool_expr
                              |      bool_expr TOK_COMMA expression_list
                              ;


assignment_right_side:               TOK_ASSIGN bool_expr
                              |      TOK_ASSIGN TOK_MULT
                                     aggregate_expression
                              |      TOK_NEW datatype
                              |      TOK_ASSIGN_INC num_expr
                              |      TOK_ASSIGN_DEC num_expr
                              |      TOK_ASSIGN_MULT num_expr
                              |      TOK_ASSIGN_DIV num_expr
                              |      TOK_ASSIGN_STRCONCAT num_expr
                              ;


free_statement:                      TOK_FREE aggregate_expression
                                     TOK_SEMICOLON
                              ;


function_table_statement:            TOK_FUNCTION_TABLE name_list
                                     TOK_SEMICOLON
                              ;


name_list:                           TOK_NAME
                              |      TOK_NAME string_constant_list
                              ;


call_table_function:                 TOK_CALL_FUNCTION TOK_LPARENTHESIS
                                     aggregate_expression TOK_COMMA num_expr
                                     TOK_RPARENTHESIS TOK_SEMICOLON
                              ;


while_statment:                      TOK_WHILE TOK_LPARENTHESIS bool_expr
                                     TOK_RPARENTHESIS stat
                              ;


do_statment:                         TOK_DO stat TOK_WHILE
                                     TOK_LPARENTHESIS bool_expr
                                     TOK_RPARENTHESIS TOK_SEMICOLON
                              ;
```

```
repeat_statement:                        TOK_REPEAT num_expr TOK_TIMES stat
                    ;


for_statement:                           TOK_FOR TOK_LPARENTHESIS TOK_NAME
                                         TOK_ASSIGN num_expr TOK_TO num_expr
                                         TOK_RPARENTHESIS stat

                    |                    TOK_FOR TOK_LPARENTHESIS TOK_NAME
                                         TOK_ASSIGN num_expr TOK_TO num_expr
                                         TOK_STEP num_expr TOK_RPARENTHESIS
                                         stat
                    ;

scan_list_statement                      TOK_SCAN_LIST TOK_LPARENTHESIS
                                         TOK_NAME TOK_IN aggregate_expression
                                         TOK_NAME TOK_RPARENTHESIS statement
                    ;
scan_db_statement                        TOK_SCAN_DB TOK_LPARENTHESIS
                                         TOK_NAME, TOK_COMMA bool_expr
                                         TOK_COMMA TOK_NAME TOK_COMMA
                                         TOK_NAME TOK_COMMA TOK_NAME
                                         TOK_RPARENTHESIS statement

                    |                    TOK_SCAN_DB TOK_LPARENTHESIS
                                         TOK_NAME, TOK_COMMA bool_expr
                                         TOK_COMMA TOK_NAME TOK_COMMA
                                         TOK_NAME TOK_RPARENTHESIS statement
                    ;

switch_statment:                         TOK_SWITCH TOK_LPARENTHESIS
                                         num_expr TOK_RPARENTHESIS
                                         TOK_LBRACE case_list TOK_RBRACE

                    |                    TOK_SWITCH TOK_LPARENTHESIS
                                         num_expr TOK_RPARENTHESIS
                                         TOK_LBRACE case_list TOK_DEFAULT
                                         TOK_COLON stat TOK_RBRACE
                    ;


case_list:                               TOK_CASE expression_list TOK_COLON stat
                    |                    TOK_CASE expression_list TOK_COLON stat
                                         case_list
                    ;


if_statement:                            TOK_IF TOK_LPARENTHESIS bool_expr
                                         TOK_RPARENTHESIS stat
```

```
                        |    TOK_IF TOK_LPARENTHESIS bool_expr
                             TOK_RPARENTHESIS stat TOK_ELSE stat
                        ;


bool_expr:                   rel_expr
                        |    rel_expr TOK_AND bool_expr
                        |    rel_expr TOK_OR bool_expr
                        |    rel_expr TOK_XOR bool_expr
                        ;


rel_expr:                    num_expr
                        |    TOK_NOT num_expr
                        |    num_expr TOK_IN TOK_LBRACE
                             expression_list TOK_RBRACE
                        |    num_expr TOK_EQ num_expr
                        |    num_expr TOK_NE num_expr
                        |    num_expr TOK_GT num_expr
                        |    num_expr TOK_GE num_expr
                        |    num_expr TOK_LT num_expr
                        |    num_expr TOK_LE num_expr
                        ;


num_expr:                    add_expr
                        |    add_expr TOK_ADDR_STRCONCAT num_expr

                        ;


add_expr:                    mult_expr
                        |    mult_expr TOK_PLUS add_expr
                        |    mult_expr TOK_SUBTRACT_MINUS add_expr
                        ;


mult_expr:                   exp_expr
                        |    exp_expr TOK_MULT mult_expr
                        |    exp_expr TOK_DIV mult_expr
                        |    exp_expr TOK_MOD mult_expr
                        ;


exp_expr:                    item_expr
                        |    item_expr TOK_POW exp_expr

                        ;
```

```
item_expr:                        TOK_LPARENTHESIS bool_expr
                                  TOK_RPARENTHESIS
                        |         TOK_SUBTRACT_MINUS item_expr
                        |         function_call dereference
                        |         aggregate_expression
                        |         TOK_INC aggregate_expression
                        |         TOK_DEC aggregate_expression
                        |         aggregate_expression TOK_INC
                        |         aggregate_expression TOK_DEC
                        |         TOK_NUMBER
                        |         TOK_NUMBER TOK_NAME
                        |         TOK_STRING_CONSTANT
                        |         TOK_DATE_CONSTANT
                        |         TOK_TIME_CONSTANT
                        |         TOK_DATETIME_CONSTANT
                        |         TOK_BOOLEAN_CONSTANT
                        ;


function_call:                    TOK_NAME TOK_LPARENTHESIS
                                  TOK_RPARENTHESIS
                        |         TOK_NAME TOK_LPARENTHESIS
                                  expression_list TOK_RPARENTHESIS
                        ;
```

Compiler directives

Compiler directives should be enclosed in '<<' '>>' characters.

The Wattleglen compiler recognises the following directives

<<external c>>   Link the Calc program to external C functions.

The Wattleglen interpreter recognises the following directives:

<<builtin 123>>   Link the Calc program to linked in C functions.

Calc compilers should parse compiler directive expressions as '<< token-
sequence >>', and implement any directives that they recognise.

Semantic overlays:

1. Control statements such as 'if', 'while' etc require an expression of 'bool' type.

2. The 'switch' statement can take a control value that is a numeric type, a string, date, time or datetime type.

3. 'For' loops require a numeric variable as the control variable.

Procedure for a 'for' loop

Calc compilers should be compatible with the following procedure:

1. Set the control variable equal to the value of the initial value expression.

2. Evaluate the end value expression.

3. Evaluate the step size expression, if any. If there is no step size expression set the step size value to +1.

4. If the step size is zero, generate a runtime error.

5. For positive step sizes:

6. Check the value of the control variable against the end value. If it is greater than the end value, jump to the next statement after the loop.

7. Execute the code inside the loop.

8. Increment the control variable by the step size.

9. Jump to step 6.

10. For negative step sizes:

11. Check the value of the control variable against the end value. If it is less than the end value, jump to the next statement after the loop.

12. Execute the code inside the loop.

13. Decrement the control variable by the step size.

14. Jump to step 11.

36. Future expansion

I have tried to make the Calc language as complete as possible.

The language is designed for application development and non-performance-critical system code such as writing compilers.

It is my hope that if it is used in the future, few if any changes will be made to the language.

Development of new compilers, libraries and tools is encouraged and appreciated.

One of the strengths of a language like C is that it has undergone almost no changes in 30 years. Similarly with SQL.

This indicates that these languages addressed their problem set in a complete way.

However other languages such as C++ are continually being expanded and made more complex, which in time might ruin them.

Having said that I have some items for future expansion.

List syntax

I would like to have the syntax x = y["item"] and y["item"] = 100 as well as calling the list functions directly.

Memory freeing

At present memory allocated using 'new' is never freed unless 'free' is manually called.

This is not a major problem for call-response models such as web pages, but it is a big potential problem for code that must run continuously.

I would like to have automatic freeing of out-of-scope memory. However this is non-trivial in Calc because Calc supports linked structures, so it is not always easy to determine which part of a structure should be freed.

#if

It would be good if the #set and #if operations supported numeric types and expressions as well as booleans.

Memory corruption

The syntax and semantics of Calc are designed so that it is possible to implement the language in such a way that memory corruptions due to errors in application code are impossible.

The current compiler is about 95% of the way there on this issue.

It would be a big win for the language if memory corruptions were impossible in Calc programs.

37. Licence

The Calc programming language is copyrighted the author, Mark McIlroy.

Licence is hereby given for the development of compilers and interpreters of the language, without licence fees.